COURAGE

How We Face Challenges

Troll Target Series

Troll

TROLL TARGET SERIES

Lewis Gardner	*Senior Editor*
Miriam Rinn	*Editor*
Virginia Pass	*Teaching Guides*
Cris Peterson	*Bibliographies*
Robert Revels	*Cover Illustration*

PROJECT CONSULTANT

David Dillon *Professor of Language Arts, McGill University, Montreal*

ACKNOWLEDGMENTS

"Tuesday of the Other June" reprinted by permission of Norma Fox Mazer. Copyright © 1986 by Norma Fox Mazer. All rights reserved.

"The Champion Who Finished Last" from *True Champions*. © 1993 by Nathan Aaseng. Reprinted with permission from Walker and Company, 435 Hudson Street, New York, New York 10014. 1-800-289-2553. All rights reserved.

(Acknowledgments continued on page 158)

Contents

Tuesday of the Other June
Norma Fox Mazer   5

The Champion Who Finished Last
Nathan Aaseng   16

74th Street
Myra Cohn Livingston   20

Zlateh the Goat
Isaac Bashevis Singer   21

Gator Aid
Editors of Time-Life Books   28

In White Tie
David Huddle   30

The Hundred Penny Box
Sharon Bell Mathis   31

Mother to Son
Langston Hughes   50

Li Chi Slays the Serpent
Kan Pao   51

Flight into Danger
Arthur Hailey   53

You've Gotta Be Kidding
Dave Barry   94

Beware: Do Not Read This Poem
Ishmael Reed   98

Lament
Edna St. Vincent Millay   100

Thurgood Marshall: The Fight for Justice
Rae Bains   101

Everything Became a Secret: Paulette Pomeranz'
  Story
Maxine Rosenberg   110

Ordeal in the Owyhee Country
Margaret Truman Daniel   116

The Middle Sister and the Tree
Corlia Fourie   128

Jimmy Valentine Reforms
Julia Remine Piggin   133

Welcome
David Hernandez   143

The Babysitter
Gary Soto   144

Why Brer Possum Has No Hair on His Tail
Julius Lester   149

Start Your Own Successful Business
Debbi Fields   152

Tuesday of the Other June

by Norma Fox Mazer

*Sometimes it takes courage just to leave your home in
the morning. June has a warm relationship with her
mother, but she needs to find her own solution to a
very big problem. How can she protect herself from a
bully—without disobeying her mother?*

"BE GOOD, BE GOOD, BE GOOD, BE GOOD, MY JUNIE," my mother said as she combed my hair; a song, a story, a croon, a plea. "It's just you and me, two women alone in the world, June darling of my heart, we have enough troubles getting by, we surely don't need a single one more, so you keep your sweet self out of fighting and all that bad stuff. People can be little-hearted, but turn the other cheek, smile at the world, and the world'll surely smile back."

We stood in front of the mirror as she combed my hair, combed and brushed and smoothed. Her head came just above mine, she said when I grew another inch she'd stand on a stool to brush my hair. "I'm not giving up this pleasure!" And she laughed her long honey laugh.

My mother was April, my grandmother had been May, I was

June. "And someday," said my mother, "you'll have a daughter of your own. What will you name her?"

"January!" I'd yell when I was little. "February! No, November!" My mother laughed her honey laugh. She had little emerald eyes that warmed me like the sun.

Every day when I went to school, she went to work. "Sometimes I stop what I'm doing," she said, "lay down my tools, and stop everything, because all I can think about is you. Wondering what you're doing and if you need me. Now, Junie, if anyone ever bothers you—"

"—I walk away, run away, come on home as fast as my feet will take me," I recited.

"Yes. You come to me. You just bring me your trouble, because I'm here on this earth to love you and take care of you."

I was safe with her. Still, sometimes I woke up at night and heard footsteps slowly creeping up the stairs. It wasn't my mother, she was asleep in the bed across the room, so it was robbers, thieves, and murderers, creeping slowly . . . slowly . . . slowly toward my bed.

I stuffed my hand into my mouth. If I screamed and woke her, she'd be tired at work tomorrow. The robbers and thieves filled the warm darkness and slipped across the floor more quietly than cats. Rigid under the covers, I stared at the shifting dark and bit my knuckles and never knew when I fell asleep again.

In the morning we sang in the kitchen. "Bill Grogan's GOAT! Was feelin' FINE! Ate three red shirts, right off the LINE!" I made sandwiches for our lunches, she made pancakes for breakfast, but all she ate was one pancake and a cup of coffee. "Gotta fly, can't be late."

I wanted to be rich and take care of her. She worked too hard, her pretty hair had gray in it that she joked about. "Someday," I said, "I'll buy you a real house and you'll never work in a pot factory again."

"Such delicious plans," she said. She checked the windows to see if they were locked. "Do you have your key?"

I lifted it from the chain around my neck.

"And you'll come right home from school and—"

"—I won't light fires or let strangers into the house and I won't tell anyone on the phone that I'm here alone," I finished for her.

"I know, I'm just your old worrywart mother." She kissed me twice, once on each cheek. "But you are my June, my only June, the only June."

She was wrong, there was another June. I met her when we stood next to each other at the edge of the pool the first day of swimming class in the Community Center.

"What's your name?" She had a deep growly voice.

"June. What's yours?"

She stared at me. "June."

"We have the same name."

"No we don't. June is *my* name, and I don't give you permission to use it. Your name is Fish Eyes." She pinched me hard. "Got it, Fish Eyes?"

The next Tuesday, the Other June again stood next to me at the edge of the pool. "What's your name?"

"June."

"Wrong. Your—name—is—Fish—Eyes."

"June."

"Fish Eyes, you are really stupid." She shoved me into the pool.

The swimming teacher looked up, frowning, from her chart. "No one in the water yet."

Later, in the locker room, I dressed quickly and wrapped my wet suit in the towel. The Other June pulled on her jeans. "You guys see that bathing suit Fish Eyes was wearing? Her mother found it in a trash can."

"She did not!"

The Other June grabbed my fingers and twisted. "Where'd she find your bathing suit?"

"She bought it, let me go."

"Poor little stupid Fish Eyes is crying. Oh, boo hoo hoo, poor little Fish Eyes."

7

After that, everyone called me Fish Eyes. And every Tuesday, wherever I was, there was also the Other June—at the edge of the pool, in the pool, in the locker room. In the water, she swam alongside me, blowing and huffing, knocking into me. In the locker room, she stepped on my feet, pinched my arms, hid my blouse, and knotted my braids together. She had large square teeth, she was shorter than I was, but heavier, with bigger bones and square hands. If I met her outside on the street, carrying her bathing suit and towel, she'd walk toward me, smiling a square, friendly smile. "Oh well, if it isn't Fish Eyes." Then she'd punch me, *blam!* her whole solid weight hitting me.

I didn't know what to do about her. She was training me like a dog. After a few weeks of this, she only had to look at me, only had to growl, "I'm going to get you, Fish Eyes," for my heart to slink like a whipped dog down into my stomach. My arms were covered with bruises. When my mother noticed, I made up a story about tripping on the sidewalk.

My weeks were no longer Tuesday, Wednesday, Thursday, and so on. Tuesday was Awfulday. Wednesday was Badday. (The Tuesday bad feelings were still there.) Thursday was Betterday and Friday was Safeday. Saturday was Goodday, but Sunday was Toosoonday, and Monday—Monday was nothing but the day before Awfulday.

I tried to slow down time. Especially on the weekends, I stayed close by my mother, doing everything with her, shopping, cooking, cleaning, going to the laundromat. "Aw, sweetie, go play with your friends."

"No, I'd rather be with you." I wouldn't look at the clock or listen to the radio (they were always telling you the date and the time). I did special magic things to keep the day from going away, rapping my knuckles six times on the bathroom door six times a day and never, ever touching the chipped place on my bureau. But always I woke up to the day before Tuesday, and always, no matter how many times I circled the worn spot in the living-room rug or counted 25 cracks in the ceiling, Monday disappeared and once again it was Tuesday.

The Other June got bored with calling me Fish Eyes. Buffalo Brain came next, but as soon as everyone knew that, she renamed me Turkey Nose.

Now at night it wasn't robbers creeping up the stairs, but the Other June, coming to torment me. When I finally fell asleep, I dreamed of kicking her, punching, biting, pinching. In the morning I remembered my dreams and felt brave and strong. And then I remembered all the things my mother had taught me and told me.

Be good, be good, be good, it's just us two women alone in the world. . . . Oh, but if it weren't, if my father wasn't long gone, if we'd had someone else to fall back on, if my mother's mother and daddy weren't dead all these years, if my father's daddy wanted to know us instead of being glad to forget us—oh, then I would have punched the Other June with a frisky heart, I would have grabbed her arm at poolside and bitten her like the dog she had made of me.

One night, when my mother came home from work, she said, "Junie, listen to this. We're moving!"

Alaska, I thought. Florida, Arizona. Someplace far away and wonderful, someplace without the Other June.

"Wait till you hear this deal. We are going to be caretakers, troubleshooters for an eight-family apartment building. Fifty-six Blue Hill Street. Not janitors, we don't do any of the heavy work. April and June, Troubleshooters, Incorporated. If a tenant has a complaint or a problem, she comes to us and we either take care of it or call the janitor for service. And for that little bit of work, we get to live rent free!" She swept me around in a dance. "Okay? You like it? I do!"

So. Not anywhere else, really. All the same, maybe too far to go to swimming class? "Can we move right away? Today?"

"Gimme a break, sweetie. We've got to pack, do a thousand things. I've got to line up someone with a truck to help us. Six weeks, Saturday the 15th." She circled it on the calendar. It was the Saturday after the last day of swimming class.

Soon, we had boxes lying everywhere, filled with clothes

and towels and glasses wrapped in newspapers. Bit by bit, we cleared the rooms, leaving only what we needed right now. The dining-room table staggered on a bunched-up rug, our bureaus inched toward the front door like patient cows. On the calendar in the kitchen, my mother marked off the days until we moved, but the only days I thought about were Tuesdays—Awfuldays. Nothing else was real except the too fast passing of time, moving toward each Tuesday . . . away from Tuesday . . . toward Tuesday . . . .

And it seemed to me that this would go on forever, that Tuesdays would come forever and I would be forever trapped by the side of the pool, the Other June whispering Buffalo Brain Fish Eyes Turkey Nose into my ear, while she ground her elbow into my side and smiled her square smile at the swimming teacher.

And then it ended. It was the last day of swimming class. The last Tuesday. We had all passed our tests and, as if in celebration, the Other June only pinched me twice. "And now," our swimming teacher said, "all of you are ready for the Advanced Class, which starts in just one month. I have a sign-up slip here. Please put your name down before you leave." Everyone but me crowded around. I went to the locker room and pulled on my clothes as fast as possible. The Other June burst through the door just as I was leaving. "Goodbye," I yelled, "good riddance to bad trash!" Before she could pinch me again, I ran past her and then ran all the way home, singing, "Good-bye . . . goodbye . . . goodbye, good riddance to bad trash!"

Later, my mother carefully untied the blue ribbon around my swimming class diploma. "Look at this! Well, isn't this wonderful! You are on your way, you might turn into an Olympic swimmer, you never know what life will bring."

"I don't want to take more lessons."

"Oh, sweetie, it's great to be a good swimmer." But then, looking into my face, she said, "No, no, no, don't worry, you don't have to."

The next morning, I woke up hungry for the first time in

weeks. No more swimming class. No more Baddays and Awfuldays. No more Tuesdays of the Other June. In the kitchen, I made hot cocoa to go with my mother's corn muffins. "It's Wednesday, Mom," I said, stirring the cocoa. "My favorite day."

"Since when?"

"Since this morning." I turned on the radio so I could hear the announcer tell the time, the temperature, and the day.

Thursday for breakfast I made cinnamon toast, Friday my mother made pancakes, and on Saturday, before we moved, we ate the last slices of bread and cleaned out the peanut butter jar.

"Some breakfast," Tilly said. "Hello, you must be June." She shook my hand. She was a friend of my mother's from work. She wore big hoop earrings, sandals, and a skirt as dazzling as a rainbow. She came in a truck with John to help us move our things.

John shouted cheerfully at me, "So you're moving." An enormous man with a face covered with little brown bumps. Was he afraid his voice wouldn't travel the distance from his mouth to my ear? "You looking at my moles?" he shouted, and he heaved our big green flowered chair down the stairs. "Don't worry, they don't bite. Ha, ha, ha!" Behind him came my mother and Tilly balancing a bureau between them, and behind them I carried a lamp and the round, flowered Mexican tray that was my mother's favorite. She had found it at a garage sale and said it was as close to foreign travel as we would ever get.

The night before, we had loaded our car, stuffing in bags and boxes until there was barely room for the two of us. But it was only when we were in the car, when we drove past Abdo's Grocery, where they always gave us credit, when I turned for a last look at our street—it was only then that I understood we were truly going to live somewhere else, in another apartment, in another place mysteriously called Blue Hill Street.

Tilly's truck followed our car.

"Oh, I'm so excited," my mother said. She laughed. "You'd think we were going across the country."

Our old car wheezed up a long, steep hill. Blue Hill Street.

11

I looked from one side to the other, trying to see everything.

My mother drove over the crest of the hill. "And now—ta da!—our new home."

"Which house? Which one?" I looked out the window and what I saw was the Other June. She was sprawled on the stoop of a pink house, lounging back on her elbows, legs outspread, her jaws working on a wad of gum. I slid down into the seat, but it was too late. I was sure she had seen me.

My mother turned into a driveway next to a big white building with a tiny porch. She leaned on the steering wheel. "See that window there, that's our living-room window . . . and that one over there, that's your bedroom. . . ."

We went into the house, down a dim, cool hall. In our new apartment, the wooden floors clicked under our shoes, and my mother showed me everything. Her voice echoed in the empty rooms. I followed her around in a daze. Had I imagined seeing the Other June? Maybe I'd seen another girl who looked like her. A double. That could happen.

"Ho yo, where do you want this chair?" John appeared in the doorway. We brought in boxes and bags and beds and stopped only to eat pizza and drink orange juice from the carton.

"June's so quiet, do you think she'll adjust all right?" I heard Tilly say to my mother.

"Oh, definitely. She'll make a wonderful adjustment. She's just getting used to things."

But I thought that if the Other June lived on the same street as I did, I would never get used to things.

That night I slept in my own bed, with my own pillow and blanket, but with floors that creaked in strange voices and walls with cracks I didn't recognize. I didn't feel either happy or unhappy. It was as if I were waiting for something.

Monday, when the principal of Blue Hill Street School left me in Mr. Morrisey's classroom, I knew what I'd been waiting for. In that room full of strange kids, there was one person I knew. She smiled her square smile, raised her hand, and said, "She can sit next to me, Mr. Morrisey."

"Very nice of you, June M. Okay, June T, take your seat. I'll try not to get you two Junes mixed up."

I sat down next to her. She pinched my arm. "Good riddance to bad trash," she mocked.

I was back in the Tuesday swimming class only now it was worse, because everyday would be Awfulday. The pinching had already started. Soon, I knew, on the playground and in the halls, kids would pass me, grinning. "Hiya, Fish Eyes."

The Other June followed me around during recess that day, droning in my ear, "You are my slave, you must do everything I say, I am your master, say it, say, 'Yes, master, you are my master.'"

I pressed my lips together, clapped my hands over my ears, but without hope. Wasn't it only a matter of time before I said the hateful words?

"How was school?" my mother said that night.

"Okay."

She put a pile of towels in a bureau drawer. "Try not to be sad about missing your old friends, sweetie, there'll be new ones."

The next morning, the Other June was waiting for me when I left the house. "Did your mother get you that blouse in the garbage dump?" She butted me, shoving me against a tree. "Don't you speak anymore, Fish Eyes?" Grabbing my chin in her hands, she pried open my mouth. "Oh, ha ha, I thought you lost your tongue."

We went on to school. I sank down into my seat, my head on my arms. "June T, are you all right?" Mr. Morrisey asked. I nodded. My head was almost too heavy to lift.

The Other June went to the pencil sharpener. Round and round she whirled the handle. Walking back, looking at me, she held the three sharp pencils like three little knives.

Someone knocked on the door. Mr. Morrisey went out into the hall. Paper planes burst into the air, flying from desk to desk. Someone turned on a transistor radio. And the Other June, coming closer, smiled and licked her lips like a cat sleepily preparing to gulp down a mouse.

13

I remembered my dream of kicking her, punching, biting her like a dog.

Then my mother spoke quickly in my ear: *Turn the other cheek, my Junie, smile at the world and the world'll surely smile back.*

But I had turned the other cheek and it was slapped. I had smiled and the world hadn't smiled back. I couldn't run home as fast as my feet would take me, I had to stay in school—and in school there was the Other June. Every morning, there would be the Other June, and every afternoon, and every day, all day, there would be the Other June.

She frisked down the aisle, stabbing the pencils in the air toward me. A boy stood up on his desk and bowed. "My fans," he said, "I greet you." My arm twitched and throbbed, as if the Other June's pencils had already poked through the skin. She came closer, smiling her Tuesday smile.

"No," I whispered, *"no."* The word took wings and flew me to my feet, in front of the Other June. *"Noooooo."* It flew out of my mouth into her surprised face.

The boy on the desk turned toward us. "You said something, my devoted fans?"

"No," I said to the Other June. "Oh, no! No. No. No. No more." I pushed away the hand that held the pencils.

The Other June's eyes opened, popped wide like the eyes of somebody in a cartoon. It made me laugh. The boy on the desk laughed, and then the other kids were laughing, too.

"No," I said again, because it felt so good to say it. "No, no, no, no." I leaned toward the Other June, put my finger against her chest. Her cheeks turned red, she squawked something—it sounded like "Eeeraaghyou!"—and she stepped back. She stepped away from me.

The door banged, the airplanes disappeared, and Mr. Morrisey walked to his desk. "Okay. Okay. Let's get back to work. Kevin Clark, how about it?" Kevin jumped off the desk and Mr. Morrisey picked up a piece of chalk. "All right, class—" He stopped and looked at me and the Other June. "You two Junes,

14

what's going on there?"

I tried it again. My finger against her chest. Then the words. "No—more." And she stepped back another step. I sat down at my desk.

"June M," Mr. Morrisey said.

She turned around, staring at him with that big-eyed cartoon look. After a moment she sat down at her desk with a loud slapping sound.

Even Mr. Morrisey laughed.

And sitting at my desk, twirling my braids, I knew this was the last Tuesday of the Other June.

The Champion Who Finished Last

by Nathan Aaseng

Champions face great odds to achieve their goals. We usually think of champions as people of great strength and skill. In this true account, we meet someone with the courage to test herself against her own limitations.

Spectators who savor a healthy dose of grit and raw determination in their sports left the finish line of the 1982 New York City Marathon feeling more than satisfied. Defending champion Alberto Salazar of the United States and Rodolfo Gomez of Mexico had waged a relentless duel the entire length of the 26.2-mile course. Neither had given an inch until Salazar finally outsprinted Gomez in the final yards of the race.

Unknown to almost all spectators and racers alike, an even more stirring tale of human spirit was unfolding far back on the course. Many miles behind the slower runners straggling into the finish area, Linda Down plodded on toward a goal still half a day's journey away.

Linda Down and her twin sister, Laura, were born in

Brooklyn in 1957 and grew up in the small town of Milford, New York. Both were born with cerebral palsy—a condition caused by brain damage that greatly restricts muscle control.

From the beginning, Linda refused to let her condition stand in the way of her curiosity. At the age of two she had to be rescued from a roof that she had reached by pulling herself up a ladder. Linda frequently fell off playground equipment that she insisted on climbing. Twice during Linda's childhood her mother dove into a swimming pool fully clothed to rescue her daughter, who had wandered into the deep end and was unable to get out.

Linda wore leg braces and had frequent surgery in an attempt to unlock her limbs from the rigid grip of cerebral palsy. But despite operations on her feet, knees, and hips, she had to rely on crutches for mobility. School insurance regulations barred her from participating in physical education activities at school. She resented not being given a chance to test her limits, and she cried when others teased her about her awkward movements. But she "decided not to be bitter because bitterness becomes a burden you carry around with you."

In the fall of 1981 Down was living in New York City with her sister when they happened to watch television coverage of the New York City Marathon. Linda, who had been thinking about getting more exercise after working hard for her masters degree in social work, commented, "Maybe we ought to try that."

Just walking down the street was an effort for Down. She moved by planting her crutches ahead of her, swinging her body weight forward on the crutches, and trying to get her twisted feet to follow. She had slightly better control over her left foot—the right foot swung out in a wider arc. She could not get either foot forward without scraping the toes over the ground.

But as time went on, Down actually began to think seriously about that absurd notion. In the spring of 1982 she began training for the October marathon.

Down battled many training obstacles that other runners never faced. No pair of running shoes could last long under the constant scraping over the sidewalks. Down suffered blisters when her feet were soaked, scraping through puddles that other runners could just hop over or sidestep. Her shoulders ached. She endured the frustration of watching other runners zip effortlessly past her while she labored at her turtle's pace. Since she could cover only about three miles per hour, putting in the necessary training for a marathon took a great deal of her time. Many workouts lasted longer than six hours. Down, who was unemployed at the time, had no time to look for a job and had to rely on her sister for financial support.

Down began to notice some of the rewards of her training as the marathon starting date drew near. She had lost weight and built up her leg muscles, and the stretching exercises had slightly relaxed her cramped muscles. But she began to wonder what she was getting herself into. "I was scared to death of running a marathon," she admitted.

Nonetheless, she showed up at the starting line wearing number W831. At 10:40 A.M., New York City mayor Ed Koch fired the starting cannon that sent more than 14,000 runners from 68 different countries off on their trek.

Linda Down was quickly left behind by even the slowest runners. As if the 26.2-mile course were not enough of a challenge, a strong head wind, gusting to nearly 25 miles per hour, battered her as she trudged by herself far to the rear of the pack. After only three miles, Down was already laboring hard, doubting that she could make it.

At that time, a small girl, one of more than two million New Yorkers who lined the course, ran up to her. The girl's face shone with excitement. "You've got to make it!" she said. The words of encouragement inspired Down to cast aside her fears of failure and to reach inside for extra determination.

Hours later, long after the leaders had finished, Down still clomped and scraped through the early part of the course. This time a boy approached her. Seeing the number on her shirt, he asked if she were a marathoner. When she told him she was, he gaped at her in astonishment. Then he patted her on the back and said, "You'll make it! Keep going!"

Linda's mom and sister followed her all of the way in a car. They supplied her with water and with oranges and candy bars for energy. Friends encouraged her along the way. A network television camera crew noticed her at about mile 10 and were so intrigued that they began following her progress, cheering her on the entire way.

Late in the afternoon, the next-to-last finisher completed the marathon. By that time, Linda Down had covered just over half the course. Spurred on by the support of her family and friends, she kept going, almost in a daze, as darkness fell upon the city. According to Down, the last 11-mile stretch "was an act of God." Hour after hour she kept up her courageous effort.

At 9:15 P.M., 11 hours and 15 minutes after setting out on her impossible journey, Linda Down crossed the finish line.

Why did she attempt to conquer such an enormous obstacle? "To test myself," she answered. "If people have learned anything from me, I hope they've learned to pursue their secret dream . . . to try something new in life, to take the risk they might not have taken."

74th Street

by Myra Cohn Livingston

Hey, this little kid gets roller skates.
She puts them on.
She stands up and almost
flops over backwards.
She sticks out a foot like
she's going somewhere and
falls down and
smacks her hand. She
grabs hold of a step to get up and
sticks out the other foot and
slides about six inches and
falls and
skins her knee.

And then, you know what?

She brushes off the dirt and the
blood and puts some
spit on it and then
sticks out the other foot

again.

Zlateh the Goat

by Isaac Bashevis Singer

For poor people in an eastern European village long ago, survival means patience, courage—and, sometimes, the help of other creatures.

At Hanukkah time the road from the village to the town is usually covered with snow, but this year the winter had been a mild one. Hanukkah had almost come, yet little snow had fallen. The sun shone most of the time. The peasants complained that because of the dry weather there would be a poor harvest of winter grain. New grass sprouted, and the peasants sent their cattle out to pasture.

For Reuven the furrier it was a bad year, and after long hesitation he decided to sell Zlateh the goat. She was old and gave little milk. Feyvel the town butcher had offered eight gulden for her. Such a sum would buy Hanukkah candles, potatoes and oil for pancakes, gifts for the children, and other holiday necessaries for the house. Reuven told his oldest boy Aaron to take the goat to town.

Aaron understood what taking the goat to Feyvel meant, but he had to obey his father. Leah, his mother, wiped the tears from her eyes when she heard the news. Aaron's younger sisters, Anna and Miriam, cried loudly. Aaron put on his quilted jacket and a cap with earmuffs, bound a rope around Zlateh's neck, and took along two slices of bread with cheese to eat on the road. Aaron was supposed to deliver the goat by evening, spend the night at the butcher's, and return the next day with the money.

While the family said good-bye to the goat, and Aaron placed the rope around her neck, Zlateh stood as patiently and good-naturedly as ever. She licked Reuven's hand. She shook her small white beard. Zlateh trusted human beings. She knew that they always fed her and never did her any harm.

When Aaron brought her out on the road to town, she seemed somewhat astonished. She'd never been led in that direction before. She looked back at him questioningly, as if to say, "Where are you taking me?" But after a while she seemed to come to the conclusion that a goat shouldn't ask questions. Still, the road was different. They passed new fields, pastures, and huts with thatched roofs. Here and there a dog barked and came running after them, but Aaron chased it away with his stick.

The sun was shining when Aaron left the village. Suddenly the weather changed. A large black cloud with a bluish center appeared in the east and spread itself rapidly over the sky. A cold wind blew in with it. The crows flew low, croaking. At first it looked as if it would rain, but instead it began to hail as in summer. It was early in the day, but it became dark as dusk. After a while the hail turned to snow.

In his twelve years Aaron had seen all kinds of weather, but he had never experienced a snow like this one. It was so dense it shut out the light of the day. In a short time their path was completely covered. The wind became as cold as ice. The road to town was narrow and winding. Aaron no longer knew where he was. He could not see through the snow. The cold soon penetrated his quilted jacket.

At first Zlateh didn't seem to mind the change in weather. She too was twelve years old and knew what winter meant. But when her legs sank deeper and deeper into the snow, she began to turn her head and look at Aaron in wonderment. Her mild eyes seemed to ask, "Why are we out in such a storm?" Aaron hoped that a peasant would come along with his cart, but no one passed by.

The snow grew thicker, falling to the ground in large, whirling flakes. Beneath it Aaron's boots touched the softness of a plowed field. He realized that he was no longer on the road. He had gone astray. He could no longer figure out which was east or west, which way was the village, the town. The wind whistled, howled, whirled the snow about in eddies. It looked as if white imps were playing tag on the fields. A white dust rose above the ground. Zlateh stopped. She could walk no longer. Stubbornly she anchored her cleft hooves in the earth and bleated as if pleading to be taken home. Icicles hung from her white beard, and her horns were glazed with frost.

Aaron did not want to admit the danger, but he knew just the same that if they did not find shelter they would freeze to death. This was no ordinary storm. It was a mighty blizzard. The snowfall had reached his knees. His hands were numb, and he could no longer feel his toes. He choked when he breathed. His nose felt like wood, and he rubbed it with snow. Zlateh's bleating began to sound like crying. Those humans in whom she had so much confidence had dragged her into a trap. Aaron began to pray to God for himself and for the innocent animal.

Suddenly he made out the shape of a hill. He wondered what it could be. Who had piled snow into such a huge heap? He moved toward it, dragging Zlateh after him. When he came near it, he realized that it was a large haystack which the snow had blanketed.

Aaron realized immediately that they were saved. With great effort he dug his way through the snow. He was a village boy and knew what to do. When he reached the hay, he hollowed out a nest for himself and the goat. No matter how cold it may

23

be outside, in the hay it is always warm, and hay was food for Zlateh. The moment she smelled it she became contented and began to eat. Outside the snow continued to fall. It quickly covered the passageway Aaron had dug. But a boy and an animal need to breathe, and there was hardly any air in their hideout. Aaron bored a kind of a window through the hay and snow and carefully kept the passage clear.

Zlateh, having eaten her fill, sat down on her hind legs and seemed to have regained her confidence in man. Aaron ate his two slices of bread and cheese, but after the difficult journey he was still hungry. He looked at Zlateh and noticed her udders were full. He lay down next to her, placing himself so that when he milked her he could squirt the milk into his mouth. It was rich and sweet. Zlateh was not accustomed to being milked that way, but she did not resist. On the contrary, she seemed eager to reward Aaron for bringing her to a shelter whose very walls, floor, and ceiling were made of food.

Through the window Aaron could catch a glimpse of the chaos outside. The wind carried before it whole drifts of snow. It was completely dark, and he did not know whether night had already come or whether it was the darkness of the storm. Thank God that in the hay it was not cold. The dried hay, grass, and field flowers exuded the warmth of the summer sun. Zlateh ate frequently; she nibbled from above, below, from the left and right. Her body gave forth an animal warmth, and Aaron cuddled up to her. He had always loved Zlateh, but now she was like a sister. He was alone, cut off from his family, and wanted to talk. He began to talk to Zlateh. "Zlateh, what do you think about what has happened to us?" he asked.

"Maaaa," Zlateh answered.

"If we hadn't found this stack of hay, we would both be frozen stiff by now," Aaron said.

"Maaaa," was the goat's reply.

"If the snow keeps on falling like this, we may have to stay here for days," Aaron explained.

"Maaaa," Zlateh bleated.

24

"What does 'Maaaa' mean?" Aaron asked. "You'd better speak up clearly."

"Maaaa. Maaaa," Zlateh tried.

"Well, let it be 'Maaaa' then," Aaron said patiently. "You can't speak, but I know you understand. I need you and you need me. Isn't that right?"

"Maaaa."

Aaron became sleepy. He made a pillow out of some hay, leaned his head on it, and dozed off. Zlateh too fell asleep.

When Aaron opened his eyes, he didn't know whether it was morning or night. The snow had blocked up his window. He tried to clear it, but when he had bored through to the length of his arm, he still hadn't reached the outside. Luckily he had his stick with him and was able to break through to the open air. It was still dark outside. The snow continued to fall and the wind wailed, first with one voice and then with many. Sometimes it had the sound of devilish laughter. Zlateh too awoke, and when Aaron greeted her, she answered, "Maaaa." Yes, Zlateh's language consisted of only one word, but it meant many things. Now she was saying, "We must accept all that God gives us—heat, cold, hunger, satisfaction, light, and darkness."

Aaron had awakened hungry. He had eaten up his food, but Zlateh had plenty of milk.

For three days Aaron and Zlateh stayed in the haystack. Aaron had always loved Zlateh, but in these three days he loved her more and more. She fed him with her milk and helped him keep warm. She comforted him with her patience. He told her many stories, and she always cocked her ears and listened. When he patted her, she licked his hand and face. Then she said, "Maaaa," and he knew it meant, I love you too.

The snow fell for three days, though after the first day it was not as thick and the wind quieted down. Sometimes Aaron felt that there could never have been a summer, that the snow had always fallen, ever since he could remember. He, Aaron, never had a father or mother or sisters. He was a snow child, born of the snow, and so was Zlateh. It was so quiet in the hay that his

25

ears rang in the stillness. Aaron and Zlateh slept all night and a good part of the day. As for Aaron's dreams, they were all about warm weather. He dreamed of green fields, trees covered with blossoms, clear brooks, and singing birds. By the third night the snow had stopped, but Aaron did not dare to find his way home in the darkness. The sky became clear and the moon shone, casting silvery nets on the snow. Aaron dug his way out and looked at the world. It was all white, quiet, dreaming dreams of heavenly splendor. The stars were large and close. The moon swam in the sky as in a sea.

On the morning of the fourth day Aaron heard the ringing of sleigh bells. The haystack was not far from the road. The peasant who drove the sleigh pointed out the way to him—not to the town and Feyvel the butcher, but home to the village. Aaron had decided in the haystack that he would never part with Zlateh.

Aaron's family and their neighbors had searched for the boy and the goat but had found no trace of them during the storm. They feared they were lost. Aaron's mother and sisters cried for him; his father remained silent and gloomy. Suddenly one of the neighbors came running to their house with the news that Aaron and Zlateh were coming up the road.

There was great joy in the family. Aaron told them how he had found the stack of hay and how Zlateh had fed him with her milk. Aaron's sisters kissed and hugged Zlateh and gave her a special treat of chopped carrots and potato peels, which Zlateh gobbled up hungrily.

Nobody ever again thought of selling Zlateh, and now that the cold weather had finally set in, the villagers needed the services of Reuven the furrier once more. When Hanukkah came, Aaron's mother was able to fry pancakes every evening, and Zlateh got her portion too. Even though Zlateh had her own pen, she often came to the kitchen, knocking on the door with her horns to indicate that she was ready to visit, and she was always admitted. In the evening, Aaron, Miriam, and Anna played dreidel. Zlateh sat near the stove watching the children and the flickering of the Hanukkah candles.

Once in a while Aaron would ask her, "Zlateh, do you remember the three days we spent together?"

And Zlateh would scratch her neck with a horn, shake her white bearded head, and come out with the single sound which expressed all her thoughts, and all her love.

Gator Aid

by the Editors of Time-Life Books

Even a 10-year-old can be a hero, when his friend is in trouble. Who, though, helps the hero?

As prelude to a fishing trip on a sultry September day in 1951, a 10-year-old, Parker Stratt of Coral Gables, Florida, and a nine-year-old girl, Jerry Gustafson, rode their bikes to an abandoned stone quarry to catch some minnows for bait. Descending a steep slope to the water's edge, Parker turned to pick up a bucket they used to dip minnows. Neither child was aware that they had become bait themselves.

Suddenly a seven-foot alligator burst from the water, sent Parker sprawling with a slap of its tail, and grasped Jerry's right arm in its jaws. Then the giant reptile backed into the water, dragging the terrified girl with it. Parker's first instinct was to reach for Jerry's hair and left arm to pull her away from the alligator, but he instantly realized that the girl's injured right arm might be torn off in such a gruesome tug-of-war. Even as he considered his options, both girl and alligator disappeared underwater. The boy waited.

Seconds later, the creature surfaced with Jerry, then rolled onto its back and momentarily lost its grip on the girl's arm. Parker was ready. Bracing his knees against the root of a tree, the boy stretched out over the water, seized Jerry by her injured right arm, and dragged the semiconscious girl out of the water. Then, as the alligator floated in the water, snapping its jaws at them, Parker pushed his companion up the pit's steep slope and out of danger.

Resting his friend in front of him on the frame of his bike, Parker rode a half mile to the Coral Gables municipal motor pool. The injured girl was put in a truck and driven to the nearest hospital, where doctors succeeded in saving her badly cut and broken arm.

Parker Stratt was immediately proclaimed a hero. A week after the fateful fishing trip, he was flown to New York to appear on national television. For months afterward, Miami area newspapers sang his praises, and he was honored by a host of organizations, including the Boy Scouts and Carnegie Hero Fund. President Harry S. Truman made Parker Stratt the recipient of the first Young American Medal for Bravery at a White House ceremony.

But to the 10-year-old boy, the title of hero became a burden as well as an honor, placing a weight of expectation that his young shoulders were not ready to bear. "My teachers and everyone looked at me differently after that," he said. "Every time we had a test in school I froze up. I made mediocre grades and I felt pretty bad about it." Thirteen years later, as a student at Dade Junior College, Stratt was still dogged by the feeling that he had not contributed anything since the day of the alligator.

Eventually he found his way into an occupation that allowed him to continue helping others in danger: Parker Stratt became a career lifeguard on a Florida beach.

In White Tie

by David Huddle

In white tie
and tails my father
danced the first two
times in his life, first
with my bride and then with
her mother. There were close
to 300 people watching, and he
kept a smile on his face, got
through it just fine. I felt
like kissing him because I'd
been through enough of a
war to know courage
when I saw it.

The Hundred Penny Box

by Sharon Bell Mathis

It isn't easy for Michael to help his great-great-aunt. He's just a little boy, and he doesn't want to defy the grown-ups around him. But he's sure he knows what she needs.

Michael sat down on the bed that used to be his and watched his great-great-aunt, Aunt Dew, rocking in the rocking chair.

He wanted to play with the hundred penny box—especially since it was raining outside—but Aunt Dew was singing that long song again. Sometimes when she sang it she would forget who he was for a whole day.

Then she would call him John.

John was his father's name. Then his mother would say, "He's Mike, Aunt Dew. His name is Michael. John's name is John. His name is Michael." But if his father was home, Aunt Dew would just say, "Where's my boy?" Then it was hard to tell whether she meant him or his father. And he would have to wait until she said something more before he knew which one she meant.

Aunt Dew didn't call his mother any name at all.

Michael had heard his father and mother talking in bed late one night. It was soon after they had come from going to Atlanta to bring back Aunt Dew. "She won't even look at me—won't call my name, nothing," his mother had said, and Michael could tell she had been crying. "She doesn't like me. I know it. I can tell. I do everything I can to make her comfortable—" His mother was crying hard. "I rode half the way across this city—all the way to Mama Dee's—to get some homemade ice cream, some decent ice cream. Mama Dee said, 'The ice cream be melted fore you get home.' So I took a cab back and made her lunch and gave her the ice cream. I sat down at the table and tried to drink my coffee—I mean, I wanted to talk to her, say something. But she sat there and ate that ice cream and looked straight ahead at the wall and never said nothing to me. She talks to Mike and if I come around she even stops talking sometime." His mother didn't say anything for a while and then he heard her say, "I care about her. But she's making me miserable in my own house."

Michael heard his father say the same thing he always said about Aunt Dew. "She's a one-hundred-year-old lady, baby." Sometimes his father would add, "And when I didn't have nobody, she was there. Look here—after Big John and Junie drowned, she gave me a home. I didn't have one. I didn't have nothing. No mother, no father, no nobody. Nobody but her. I've loved her all my life. Like I love you. And that tough beautiful boy we made—standing right outside the door and listening for all he's worth—and he's supposed to be in his room asleep."

Michael remembered he had run back to his room and gotten back into bed and gotten up again and tip-toed over to the bedroom door to close it a little and shut off some of the light shining from the bathroom onto Aunt Dew's face. Then he looked at Aunt Dew and wished she'd wake up and talk to him like she did when she felt like talking and telling him all kinds of stories about people.

"Hold tight, Ruth," he had heard his father say that night.

"She knows we want her. She knows it. And baby, baby—sweet woman, you doing fine. Everything you doing is right." Then Michael could hear the covers moving where his mother and father were and he knew his father was putting his arms around his mother because sometimes he saw them still asleep in the morning and that's the way they looked.

But he was tired of remembering now and he was tired of Aunt Dew singing and singing and singing.

"Aunt Dew," Michael whispered close to his great-great-aunt's wrinkled face. "Can we play with the hundred penny box?"

"Precious Lord—"

"Aunt Dew! Let's count the pennies out."

"Take my hand—"

"Aunt Dew!"

"Lead me on—"

Michael thought for a moment. He knew the large scratched wooden box was down beside the dresser, on the floor where he could easily get it.

Except it was no fun to count the pennies alone.

It was better when Aunt Dew whacked him a little and said, "Stop right there, boy. You know what that penny means?" And he'd say, "You tell me," and she would tell him.

But when she started singing it was hard to stop her. At least when she was dancing what she called "moving to the music," she'd get tired after a while. Then she would tell him about the pennies and help count them too.

Michael cupped his large hands—everybody talked about how large his hands were for his age—around his great-great-aunt's ear. "Aunt Dew!" he said loudly.

Aunt Dew stopped rocking hard and turned and looked at him. But he didn't say anything and she didn't say anything. Aunt Dew turned her head and began to sing again. Exactly where she had left off. *"Let me stand—"*

Michael moved away from the rocking chair and sat back down on the bed. Then he got up and went to the dresser. He reached down and picked up the heavy, scratched-up hundred

33

penny box from the floor, walked to the bedroom door, and stood there for a moment before he went out.

There was no way to stop Aunt Dew once she started singing that long song.

Michael walked down the hall and held the huge box against his stomach. He could still hear Aunt Dew's high voice.

"I am weak. I am worn."

"What's wrong?" his mother asked when he walked into the kitchen and sat down on a chair and stared at the floor.

He didn't want to answer.

"Oh," his mother said and reached for the hundred penny box in his arms. "Give me that thing," she said. "That goes today! Soon as Aunt Dew's asleep, that goes in the furnace."

Michael almost jumped out of the chair. He wouldn't let go of the big, heavy box. He could hear his great-great-aunt's voice. She was singing louder. *"Lead me through the night, precious Lord. Take my hand."*

"You can't take the hundred penny box," Michael cried. "I'll tell Daddy if you take it and burn it up in the furnace like you burned up all the rest of Aunt Dew's stuff!" Then Michael thought of all the things he and Aunt Dew had hidden in his closet, and almost told his mother.

His mother walked closer to him and stood there but he wasn't afraid. Nobody was going to take Aunt Dew's hundred penny box. Nobody. Nobody. Nobody.

"Aunt Dew's like a child," his mother said quietly. "She's like you. Thinks she needs a whole lot of stuff she really doesn't. I'm not taking her pennies—you know I wouldn't take her pennies. I'm just getting rid of that big old ugly wooden box always under foot!"

Michael stood up. "No," he said.

"Mike, did you say no to me?" his mother asked. She put her hands on her hips.

"I mean," Michael said and tried to think fast. "Aunt Dew won't go to sleep if she doesn't see her box in the corner. Can I take it back and then you can let her see it? And when she goes

34

to sleep, you can take it."

"Go put it back in her room then," his mother said. "I'll get it later."

"Okay," Michael said and held the heavy box tighter and walked slowly back down the hall to the small bedroom that used to be his. He opened the door and went in, put the hundred penny box down on the floor and sat down on it, staring at his aunt. She wasn't singing, just sitting. "John-boy," she said.

"Yes, Aunt Dew," Michael answered and didn't care this time that she was calling him John again. He was trying to think.

"Put my music on."

The music wasn't going to help him think because the first thing she was going to do was to make him "move" too.

But Michael got off the hundred penny box and reached under his bed and pulled out his blue record player that he had got for his birthday. He had already plugged it in the wall when he heard her say, "Get mine. My own Victrola, the one your father give me."

"Momma threw it out," Michael said and knew he had told her already, a lot of times. "It was broken."

Aunt Dew squeezed her lips real tight together. "Your momma gonna throw me out soon," she said.

Michael stood still and stared at his great-great-aunt. "Momma can't throw *people* out," he said.

"Put my music on, boy," Aunt Dew said again. "And be quick about it."

"Okay," Michael said and turned the record player on and got the record, Aunt Dew's favorite, that they had saved and hidden in the bottom drawer.

The dusty, chipped record was of a lady singing that long song, *"Precious Lord, Take My Hand."* Michael turned it down low.

Aunt Dew started humming and Michael sat down on the bed and tried to think about what he'd do with the hundred penny box.

Aunt Dew got up from her rocking chair and stood up. She kept her arms down by her sides and made her thin hands into fists and clenched her lips tight and moved real slow in one spot. Her small shoulders just went up and down and up and down. "Get up, John-boy," she said, "and move with me. Move with Dewbet Thomas!"

"I don't feel like dancing," Michael said and kept sitting on the bed. But he watched his great-great-aunt move both her thin arms to one side and then to the other and move her hands about and hold her dress. Then she stopped and started all of a sudden again, just swinging her arms and moving her shoulders up and down and singing some more. Every time the record ended, he'd start it again.

When he was playing it for the third time, he said, "Aunt Dew, where will you put your hundred pennies if you lose your hundred penny box?"

"When I lose my hundred penny box, I lose me," she said and kept moving herself from side to side and humming.

"I mean maybe you need something better than an old cracked-up, wacky-dacky box with the top broken."

"It's *my* old cracked-up, wacky-dacky box with the top broken," Aunt Dew said. And Michael saw her move her shoulders real high that time. "Them's my years in that box," she said. "That's me in that box."

"Can I hide the hundred penny box, Aunt Dew," Michael asked, hoping she'd say yes and not ask him why. He'd hide it like the other stuff she had asked him to and had even told him where to hide it most of the time.

"No, don't hide my hundred penny box!" Aunt Dew said out loud. "Leave my hundred penny box right alone. Anybody take my hundred penny box takes me!"

"Just in case," Michael said impatiently and wished his great-great-aunt would sit back down in her chair so he could talk to her. "Just in case Momma puts it in the furnace when you go to sleep like she puts all your stuff in the furnace in the basement."

"What your momma name?"

36

"Oh, no," Michael said. "You keep *on* forgetting Momma's name!" That was the only thing bad about being a hundred years old like Aunt Dew—you kept *on* forgetting things that were important.

"Hush, John-boy," Aunt Dew said and stopped dancing and humming and sat back down in the chair and put the quilt back over her legs.

"You keep on forgetting."

"I don't."

"You do, you keep on forgetting!"

"Do I forget to play with you when you worry me to death to play?"

Michael didn't answer.

"Do I forget to play when you want?"

"No."

"Okay. What your momma name? Who's that in my kitchen?"

"Momma's name is Ruth, but this isn't your house. Your house is in Atlanta. We went to get you and now you live with us."

"Ruth."

Michael saw Aunt Dew staring at him again. Whenever she stared at him like that, he never knew what she'd say next. Sometimes it had nothing to do with what they had been talking about.

"You John's baby," she said, still staring at him. "Look like John just spit you out."

"That's my father."

"My great-nephew," Aunt Dew said. "Only one ever care about me." Aunt Dew rocked hard in her chair then and Michael watched her. He got off the bed and turned off the record player and put the record back into the bottom drawer. Then he sat down on the hundred penny box again.

"See that tree out there?" Aunt Dew said and pointed her finger straight toward the window with the large tree pressed up against it. Michael knew exactly what she'd say.

"Didn't have no puny-looking trees like that near my house," she said. "Dewbet Thomas—that's me, and Henry Thomas—that was my late husband, had the biggest, tallest, prettiest trees and the widest yard in all Atlanta. And John, that was your daddy, liked it most because he was city and my five sons, Henry, Jr., and Truke and Latt and the twins—Booker and Jay—well, it didn't make them no never mind because it was always there. But when my oldest niece Junie and her husband—we called him Big John—brought your daddy down to visit every summer, they couldn't get the suitcase in the house good before he was climbing up and falling out the trees. We almost had to feed him up them trees!"

"Aunt Dew, we have to hide the box."

"Junie and Big John went out on that water and I was feeling funny all day. Didn't know what. Just feeling funny. I told Big John, I said, 'Big John, that boat old. Nothing but a piece a junk.' But he fooled around and said, 'We taking it out.' I looked and saw him and Junie on that water. Then it wasn't nothing. Both gone. And the boat turned over, going downstream. Your daddy, brand-new little britches on, just standing there looking, wasn't saying nothing. No hollering. I try to give him a big hunk of potato pie. But he just looking at me, just looking and standing. Wouldn't eat none of that pie. Then I said, 'Run get Henry Thomas and the boys.' He looked at me and then he looked at that water. He turned round real slow and walked toward the west field. He never run. All you could see was them stiff little britches—red they was—moving through the corn. Bare-waisted, he was. When we found the boat later, he took it clean apart—what was left of it—every plank, and pushed it back in that water. I watched him. Wasn't a piece left of that boat. Not a splinter."

"Aunt Dew, where can we hide the box!"

"What box?"

"The hundred penny box."

"We can't hide the hundred penny box and if she got to take my hundred penny box—she might as well take me!"

"We have to hide it!"

"No—'we' don't. It's *my* box!"

"It's *my* house. And I said we have to hide it!"

"How you going to hide a house, John?"

"Not the house! Our hundred penny box!"

"It's *my* box!"

Michael was beginning to feel desperate. But he couldn't tell her what his mother had said. "Suppose Momma takes it when you go to sleep?"

Aunt Dew stopped rocking and stared at him again. "Like John just spit you out," she said. "Go on count them pennies, boy. Less you worry me in my grave if you don't. Dewbet Thomas's hundred penny box. Dewbet Thomas a hundred years old and I got a penny to prove it—each year!"

Michael got off the hundred penny box and sat on the floor by his great-great-aunt's skinny feet stuck down inside his father's old slippers. He pulled the big wooden box toward him and lifted the lid and reached in and took out the small cloth roseprint sack filled with pennies. He dumped the pennies out into the box.

He was about to pick up one penny and put it in the sack, the way they played, and say "One," when his great-great-aunt spoke.

"Why you want to hide my hundred penny box?"

"To play," Michael said, after he thought for a moment.

"Play now," she said. "Don't hide my hundred penny box. I got to keep looking at my box and when I don't see my box I won't see me neither."

"One!" Michael said and dropped the penny back into the old print sack.

"18 and 74," Aunt Dew said. "Year I was born. Slavery over! Black men in Congress running things. They was in charge. It was the Reconstruction."

Michael counted twenty-seven pennies back into the old print sack before she stopped talking about Reconstruction. "19 and 01," Aunt Dew said. "I was twenty-seven years. Birthed my twin boys. Hattie said, 'Dewbet, you got two babies.' I asked

Henry Thomas, I said, 'Henry Thomas, what them boys look like?' "

By the time Michael had counted fifty-six pennies, his mother was standing at the door.

"19 and 30," Aunt Dew said. "Depression. Henry Thomas, that was my late husband, died. Died after he put the fifty-six penny in my box. He had the double pneumonia and no decent shoes and he worked too hard. Said he was going to sweat the trouble out his lungs. Couldn't do it. Same year I sewed that fancy dress for Rena Coles. She want a hundred bows all over that dress. I was sewing bows and tieing bows and twisting bows and cursing all the time. Was her *fourth* husband and she want a dress full of bow-ribbons. Henry the one started that box, you know. Put the first thirty-one pennies in it for me and it was my birthday. After fifty-six, I put them all in myself."

"Aunt Dew, time to go to bed," his mother said, standing at the door.

"Now, I'm not sleepy," Aunt Dew said. "John-boy and me just talking. Why you don't call him John? Look like John just spit him out. Why you got to call that boy something different from his daddy?"

Michael watched his mother walk over and open the window wide. "We'll get some fresh air in here," she said. "And then, Aunt Dew, you can take your nap better and feel good when you wake up." Michael wouldn't let his mother take the sack of pennies out of his hand. He held tight and then she let go.

"I'm not sleepy," Aunt Dew said again. "This child and me just talking."

"I know," his mother said, pointing her finger at him a little. "But we're just going to take our nap anyway."

"I got a long time to sleep and I ain't ready now. Just leave me sit here in this little narrow piece a room. I'm not bothering nobody."

"Nobody said you're bothering anyone but as soon as I start making that meat loaf, you're going to go to sleep in your chair and fall out again and hurt yourself and John'll wonder where I was and say I was on the telephone and that'll be something all over again."

"Well, I'll sit on the floor and if I fall, I'll be there already and it won't be nobody's business but my own."

"Michael," his mother said and took the sack of pennies out of his hand and laid it on the dresser. Then she reached down and closed the lid of the hundred penny box and pushed it against the wall. "Go out the room, honey, and let Momma help Aunt Dew into bed."

"I been putting Dewbet Thomas to bed a long time and I can still do it," Aunt Dew said.

"I'll just help you a little," Michael heard his mother say through the closed door.

As soon as his mother left the room, he'd go in and sneak out the hundred penny box.

But where would he hide it?

Michael went into the bathroom to think, but his mother came in to get Aunt Dew's washcloth. "Why are you looking like that?" she asked. "If you want to play, go in my room. Play there, or in the living room. And don't go bothering Aunt Dew. She needs her rest."

Michael went into his father's and his mother's room and lay down on the big king bed and tried to think of a place to hide the box.

He had an idea!

He'd hide it down in the furnace room and sneak Aunt Dew downstairs to see it so she'd know where it was. Then maybe they could sit on the basement steps inside and play with it sometimes. His mother would never know. And his father wouldn't care as long as Aunt Dew was happy. He could even show Aunt Dew the big pipes and the little pipes.

Michael heard his mother close his bedroom door and walk down the hall toward the kitchen.

He'd tell Aunt Dew right now that they had a good place to hide the hundred penny box. The best place of all.

Michael got down from the huge bed and walked quietly back down the hall to his door and knocked on it very lightly. Too lightly for his mother to hear.

Aunt Dew didn't answer.

"Aunt Dew," he whispered after he'd opened the door and tiptoed up to the bed. "It's me. Michael."

Aunt Dew was crying.

Michael looked at his great-great-aunt and tried to say something but she just kept crying. She looked extra small in his bed and the covers were too close about her neck. He moved them down a little and then her face didn't look so small. He waited to see if she'd stop crying but she didn't. He went out of the room and down the hall and stood near his mother. She was chopping up celery. "Aunt Dew's crying," he said.

"That's all right," his mother said. "Aunt Dew's all right."

"She's crying real hard."

"When you live long as Aunt Dew's lived, honey—sometimes you just cry. She'll be all right."

"She's not sleepy. You shouldn't make her go to sleep if she doesn't want to. Daddy never makes her go to sleep."

"You say you're not sleepy either, but you always go to sleep."

"Aunt Dew's bigger than me!"

"She needs her naps."

"Why?"

"Michael, go play please," his mother said. "I'm tired and I'm busy and she'll hear your noise and never go to sleep."

"She doesn't have to if she doesn't want!" Michael yelled and didn't care if he did get smacked. "We were just playing and then you had to come and make her cry!"

"Without a nap, she's irritable and won't eat. She has to eat. She'll get sick if she doesn't eat."

"You made her cry!" Michael yelled.

"Michael John Jefferson," his mother said too quietly. "If you don't get away from me and stop that yelling and stop that screaming and leave me alone—!"

Michael stood there a long time before he walked away.

"Mike," his mother called but he didn't answer. All he did was stop walking.

His mother came down the hall and put her arm about him and hugged him a little and walked him back into the kitchen.

Michael walked very stiffly. He didn't feel like any hugging. He wanted to go back to Aunt Dew.

"Mike," his mother said, leaning against the counter and still holding him.

Michael let his mother hold him but he didn't hold her back. All he did was watch the pile of chopped celery.

"Mike, I'm going to give Aunt Dew that tiny mahogany chest your daddy made in a woodshop class when he was a teen-ager. It's really perfect for that little sack of pennies and when she sees it on that pretty dresser scarf she made—the one I keep on my dresser—she'll like it just as well as that big old clumsy box. She won't even miss that big old ugly thing!"

"The hundred penny box isn't even *bothering* you!"

His mother didn't answer. But Michael heard her sigh. "You don't even care about Aunt Dew's stuff," Michael yelled a little. He even pulled away from his mother. He didn't care at all about her hugging him. Sometimes it seemed to him that grown-ups never cared about anything unless it was theirs and nobody else's. He wasn't going to be like that when he grew up and could work and could do anything he wanted to do.

"Mike," his mother said quietly. "Do you remember that teddy bear you had? The one with the crooked head? We could never sit him up quite right because of the way you kept him bent all the time. You'd bend him up while you slept with him at night and bend him up when you hugged him, played with him. Do you remember that, Mike?"

Why did she have to talk about a dumb old teddy bear!

"You wouldn't let us touch that teddy bear. I mean it was all torn up and losing its stuffing all over the place. And your daddy wanted to get rid of it and I said, 'No. Mike will let us know when he doesn't need that teddy bear anymore.' So you held

43

onto that teddy bear and protected it from all kinds of monsters and people. Then, one day, you didn't play with it anymore. I think it was when little Corky moved next door."

"Corky's not little!"

"I'm sorry. Yes—Corky's big. He's a very big boy. But Corky wasn't around when you and I cleaned up your room a little while back. We got rid of a lot of things so that Aunt Dew could come and be more comfortable. That day, you just tossed that crooked teddy bear on top of the heap and never even thought about it—"

"I *did* think about it," Michael said.

"But you knew you didn't need it anymore," his mother whispered and rubbed his shoulder softly. "But it's not the same with Aunt Dew. She will hold onto everything that is hers—just hold onto them! She will hold them tighter and tighter and she will not go forward and try to have a new life. This is a new life for her, Mike. You must help her have this new life and not just let her go backward to something she can never go back to. Aunt Dew does *not* need that huge, broken, half-rotten wooden box that you stumble all over the house with—just to hold one tiny little sack of pennies!"

"I don't stumble around with it!"

His mother reached down then and kissed the top of his head. "You're the one that loves that big old box, Mike. I think that's it."

Michael felt the kiss in his hair and he felt her arms about him and he saw the pile of celery. His mother didn't understand. She didn't understand what a hundred penny box meant. She didn't understand that a new life wasn't very good if you had to have everything old taken away from you—just for a dumb little stupid old funny-looking ugly little red box, a shiny ugly nothing box that didn't even look like it was big enough to hold a sack of one hundred pennies!

Mike put his arms around his mother. Maybe he could make her understand. He hugged her hard. That's what she had done—hugged him. "All Aunt Dew wants is her hundred penny box," Michael said. "That's the only thing—"

"And all you wanted was that teddy bear," his mother answered.

"You can't burn it," Michael said and moved away from his mother. "You can't burn any more of Aunt Dew's stuff. You can't take the hundred penny box. I said you can't take it!"

"Okay," his mother said.

Michael went down the hall and opened the door to his room.

"No, Mike," his mother said and hurried after him. "Don't go in there now."

"I am," Michael said.

His mother snatched him and shut the door and pulled him into the living room and practically threw him into the stuffed velvet chair. "You're as stubborn as your father," she said. "Everything your way or else!" She was really angry. "Just sit there," she said. "And don't move until I tell you!"

As soon as Michael heard his mother chopping celery again, he got up from the chair.

He tiptoed into his room and shut the door without a sound.

Aunt Dew was staring at the ceiling. There was perspiration on her forehead and there was water in the dug-in places around her eyes.

"Aunt Dew?"

"What you want, John-boy?"

"I'm sorry Momma's mean to you."

"Ain't nobody mean to Dewbet Thomas—cause Dewbet Thomas ain't mean to nobody," Aunt Dew said, and reached her hand out from under the cover and patted Michael's face. "Your Momma Ruth. She move around and do what she got to do. First time I see her—I say, 'John, she look frail but she ain't.' He said, 'No, she ain't frail.' I make out like I don't see her all the time," Aunt Dew said, and winked her eye. "But she know I see her. If she think I don't like her that ain't the truth. Dewbet Thomas like everybody. But me and her can't talk like me and John

45

talk—cause she don't know all what me and John know."

"I closed the door," Michael said. "You don't have to sleep if you don't want to."

"I been sleep all day, John," Aunt Dew said.

Michael leaned over his bed and looked at his great-great-aunt. "You haven't been sleep all day," he said. "You've been sitting in your chair and talking to me and then you were dancing to your record and then we were counting pennies and we got to fifty-six and then Momma came."

"Where my hundred penny box?"

"I got it," Michael answered.

"Where you got it?"

"Right here by the bed."

"Watch out while I sleep."

He'd tell her about the good hiding place later. "Okay," he said.

Aunt Dew was staring at him. "Look like John just spit you out," she said.

Michael moved away from her. He turned his back and leaned against the bed and stared at the hundred penny box. All of a sudden it looked real *real* old and beat up.

"Turn round. Let me look at you."

Michael turned around slowly and looked at his great-great-aunt.

"John!"

"It's me," Michael said. "Michael."

He went and sat down on the hundred penny box.

"Come here so I can see you," Aunt Dew said.

Michael didn't move.

"Stubborn like your daddy. Don't pay your Aunt Dew no never mind!"

Michael still didn't get up.

"Go on back and do your counting out my pennies. Start with fifty-seven—where you left off. 19 and 31. Latt married that schoolteacher. We roasted three pigs. Just acting the fool, everybody. Latt give her a pair of yellow shoes for her birthday.

46

Walked off down the road one evening just like you please, she did. Had on them yellow shoes. Rode a freight train clean up to Chicago. Left his food on the table and all his clothes ironed. Six times she come back and stay for a while and then go again. Truke used to say, 'Wouldn't be *my* wife.' But Truke never did marry nobody. Only thing he care about was that car. He would covered it with a raincoat when it rained, if he could."

"First you know me, then you don't," Michael said.

"Michael John Jefferson what your name is," Aunt Dew said. "Should be plain John like your daddy and your daddy's daddy— stead of all this new stuff. Name John and everybody saying 'Michael.'" Aunt Dew was smiling. "Come here, boy," she said. "Come here close. Let me look at you. Got a head full of hair."

Michael got up from the hundred penny box and stood at the foot of the bed.

"Get closer," Aunt Dew said.

Michael did.

"Turn these covers back little more. This little narrow piece a room don't have the air the way my big house did."

"I took a picture of your house," Michael said and turned the covers back some more.

"My house bigger than your picture," Aunt Dew said. "Way bigger."

Michael leaned close to her on his bed and propped his elbows up on the large pillow under her small head. "Tell me about the barn again," he said.

"Dewbet and Henry Thomas had the biggest, reddest barn in all Atlanta, G-A!"

"And the swing Daddy broke," Michael asked and put his head down on the covers. Her chest was so thin under the thick quilt that he hardly felt it. He reached up and pushed a few wispy strands of her hair away from her closed eyes.

"Did more pulling it down than he did swinging."

"Tell me about the swimming pool," Michael said. He touched Aunt Dew's chin and covered it up with only three fingers.

47

It was a long time before Aunt Dew answered. "Wasn't no swimming pool," she said. "I done told you was a creek. Plain old creek. And your daddy like to got bit by a cottonmouth."

"Don't go to sleep, Aunt Dew," Michael said. "Let's talk."

"I'm tired, John."

"I can count the pennies all the way to the end if you want me to."

"Go head and count."

"When your hundred and one birthday comes, I'm going to put in the new penny like you said."

"Yes, John."

Michael reached up and touched Aunt Dew's eyes. "I have a good place for the hundred penny box, Aunt Dew," he said quietly.

"Go way. Let me sleep," she said.

"You wish you were back in your own house, Aunt Dew?"

"I'm going back," Aunt Dew said.

"You sad?"

"Hush, boy!"

Michael climbed all the way up on the bed and put his whole self alongside his great-great-aunt. He touched her arms. "Are your arms a hundred years old?" he asked. It was their favorite question game.

"Um-hm," Aunt Dew murmured and turned a little away from him.

Michael touched her face. "Is your face and your eyes and fingers a hundred years old too?"

"John, I'm tired," Aunt Dew said. "Don't talk so."

"How do you get to be a hundred years old?" Michael asked and raised up from the bed on one elbow and waited for his great-great-aunt to answer.

"First you have to have a hundred penny box," his great-great-aunt finally said.

"Where you get it from?" Michael asked.

"Somebody special got to give it to you," Aunt Dew said. "And soon as they give it to you, you got to be careful less it disappear."

48

"Aunt Dew—"

"Precious Lord—"

"Aunt Dew?"

"Take my hand—"

Michael put his head down on Aunt Dew's thin chest beneath the heavy quilt and listened to her sing her long song.

Mother to Son

by Langston Hughes

Well, son, I'll tell you:
Life for me ain't been no crystal stair.
It's had tacks in it,
And splinters,
And boards torn up,
And places with no carpet on the floor—
Bare.
But all the time
I'se been a-climbin' on,
And reachin' landin's,
And turnin' corners,
And sometimes goin' in the dark
Where there ain't been no light.
So, boy, don't you turn back.
Don't set down on the steps
'Cause you find it kinder hard.
Don't you fall now—
For I'se still goin', honey,
I'se still climbin',
And life for me ain't been no crystal stair.

Li Chi Slays the Serpent

by Kan Pao

*In this folktale from China, Li Chi proves that
daughters are valuable to their families and to society.
With courage and cleverness, even a giant serpent can
be defeated.*

In Fukien, in the ancient state of Yüeh, stands the Yung
mountain range, whose peaks sometimes reach a height of
many miles. To the northwest there is a cleft in the
mountains once inhabited by a giant serpent 70 or 80 feet long
and wider than the span of ten hands. It kept the local people
in a state of constant terror and had already killed many
commandants from the capital city and many magistrates and
officers of nearby towns. Offerings of oxen and sheep did not
appease the monster. By entering men's dreams and making its
wishes known through mediums, it demanded young girls of 12
or 13 to feast on.

Helpless, the commandant and the magistrates selected
daughters of bondmaids or criminals and kept them until the
appointed dates. One day in the eighth month of every year,

they would deliver a girl to the mouth of the monster's cave, and the serpent would come out and swallow the victim. This continued for nine years until nine girls had been devoured.

In the tenth year the officials had again begun to look for a girl to hold in readiness for the appointed time. A man of Chiang Lo county, Li Tan, had raised six daughters and no sons. Chi, his youngest girl, responded to the search for a victim by volunteering. Her parents refused to allow it, but she said, "Dear parents, you have no one to depend on, for having brought forth six daughters and not a single son, it is as if you were childless. I could never compare with Ti Jung of the Han Dynasty, who offered herself as a bondmaid to the emperor in exchange for her father's life. I cannot take care of you in your old age; I only waste your food and clothes. Since I'm no use to you alive, why shouldn't I give up my life a little sooner? What could be wrong in selling me to gain a bit of money for yourself?" But the father and mother loved her too much to consent, so she went in secret.

The volunteer then asked the authorities for a sharp sword and a snake-hunting dog. When the appointed day of the eighth month arrived, she seated herself in the temple, clutching the sword and leading the dog. First she took several pecks of rice balls moistened with malt sugar and placed them at the mouth of the serpent's cave.

The serpent appeared. Its head was as large as a rice barrel; its eyes were like mirrors two feet across. Smelling the fragrance of the rice balls, it opened its mouth to eat them. Then Li Chi unleashed the snake-hunting dog, which bit hard into the serpent. Li Chi herself came up from behind and scored the serpent with several deep cuts. The wounds hurt so terribly that the monster leaped into the open and died.

Li Chi went into the serpent's cave and recovered the skulls of the nine victims. She sighed as she brought them out, saying, "For your timidity you were devoured. How pitiful!" Slowly she made her way homeward.

Flight into Danger

by Arthur Hailey

In the early days of television, plays were presented "live," not on film or videotape. Scenes were broadcast from several locations in a studio. Sometimes, in this script from the 1950s, film is used to show the outside of the airplane or the airport, but all the other action takes place in studio settings. In this way the story is told of George Spencer's heroic efforts to land an airliner on its flight across western Canada.

CHARACTERS

Aboard Flight 714:

The Passengers:	GEORGE SPENCER
	DR. FRANK BAIRD
	SEVEN MALE PASSENGERS
	TWO WOMEN PASSENGERS
The Crew:	CAPTAIN
	FIRST OFFICER
	STEWARDESS

At Vancouver Airport:

CAPTAIN MARTIN TRELEAVEN	SWITCHBOARD OPERATOR
AIRPORT CONTROLLER	RADIO OPERATOR
HARRY BURDICK	TOWER CONTROLLER

At Winnipeg Airport:

FIRST PASSENGER AGENT	SECOND PASSENGER AGENT

ACT I

FADE IN: *the passenger lobby of Winnipeg Air Terminal at night. At the departure counter of Cross-Canada Airlines a male passenger agent in uniform* [FIRST AGENT] *is checking a manifest. He reaches for p.a. mike.*

FIRST AGENT: Flight 98, direct fleet-liner service to Vancouver, with connections for Victoria, Seattle, and Honolulu, leaving immediately through gate four. No smoking. All aboard, please.

> [*During the announcement* GEORGE SPENCER *enters through the main lobby doorway. About 35, he is a senior factory salesman for a motor truck manufacturer.* SPENCER *pauses to look for the Cross-Canada counter, then hastens toward it, arriving as the announcement concludes.*]

SPENCER: Is there space on Flight 98 for Vancouver?

FIRST AGENT: Sorry, sir, that flight is full. Did you check with Reservations?

SPENCER: Didn't have time. I came straight out on the chance you might have a "no show" seat.

FIRST AGENT: With the big football game on tomorrow in Vancouver, I don't think you'll have much chance of getting out before tomorrow afternoon.

SPENCER: That's no good. I've got to be in Vancouver tomorrow by midday.

FIRST AGENT [*hesitates*]: Look, I'm not supposed to tell you this, but there's a charter flight in from Toronto. They're going out to the coast for the game. I did hear they were a few seats light.

SPENCER: Who's in charge? Where do I find him?

FIRST AGENT: Ask at the desk over there. They call themselves Maple Leaf Air Charter. But mind, *I* didn't send you.

SPENCER [*smiles*]: Okay, thanks. [SPENCER *crosses to another departure counter which has a cardboard sign hanging behind it—Maple Leaf Air Charter. Behind the desk is an agent in a lounge suit. He is checking a manifest.*] Excuse me.

SECOND AGENT: Yes?

SPENCER: I was told you might have space on a flight to Vancouver.

SECOND AGENT: Yes, there's one seat left. The flight's leaving right away though.

SPENCER: That's what I want.

SECOND AGENT: Very well, sir. Your name, please?

SPENCER: Spencer—George Spencer.

SECOND AGENT: That'll be 55 dollars for the one-way trip.

SPENCER: Will you take my air-travel card?

SECOND AGENT: No sir. Just old-fashioned cash.

SPENCER: All right. [*Produces wallet and counts out bills.*]

SECOND AGENT [*handing over ticket*]**:** Do you have any bags?

SPENCER: One. Right here.

SECOND AGENT: All the baggage is aboard. Would you mind keeping that with you?

SPENCER: Be glad to.

SECOND AGENT: Okay, Mr. Spencer. Your ticket is your boarding pass. Go through gate three and ask the commissionaire for Flight 714. Better hurry.

SPENCER: Thanks a lot. Good night.

SECOND AGENT: Good night. [*Exit* SPENCER. *Enter* STEWARDESS.] Hi, Janet. Did the meals get aboard?

STEWARDESS: Yes, they've just put them on. What was the trouble?

SECOND AGENT: Couldn't get service from the regular caterers here. We had to go to some outfit the other side of town. That's what held us up.

STEWARDESS: Are we all clear now?

SECOND AGENT: Yes, here's everything you'll need. [*Hands over papers.*] There's one more passenger. He's just gone aboard. So that's 56 souls in your lovely little hands.

STEWARDESS: I'll try not to drop any.

SECOND AGENT [*reaching for coat*]**:** Well, I'm off home.

STEWARDESS [*as she leaves*]**:** 'Night.

SECOND AGENT [*pulling on coat*]**:** 'Night, Janet. [*Calls after* *her.*] Don't forget to cheer for the Blue Bombers tomorrow.

> [STEWARDESS *waves and smiles.*
>
> [DISSOLVE TO: *the passenger cabin of a DC-4 liner. There is one empty aisle seat. Seated next to it is* DR. FRANK BAIRD, M.D., *55.* GEORGE SPENCER *enters, sees the unoccupied seat and comes toward it.*]

SPENCER: Pardon me, is this anyone's seat?

BAIRD: No.

SPENCER: Thanks. [SPENCER *sheds his topcoat and puts it on the rack above the seats. Meanwhile the plane's motors can be heard starting.*

> [CUT TO: FILM INSERT—*four-engined airplane exterior, night: the motors starting.*
>
> [CUT TO: *the passenger cabin.*]

BAIRD: I presume you're going to the big game like the rest of us.

SPENCER: I'm ashamed to admit it, but I'd forgotten about the game.

BAIRD: I wouldn't say that too loudly if I were you. Some of the more exuberant fans might tear you limb from limb.

SPENCER: I'll keep my voice down. [*Pleasantly.*] Matter of fact, I'm making a sales trip to the coast.

BAIRD: What do you sell?

SPENCER: Trucks.

BAIRD: Trucks?

SPENCER: That's right. I'm what the local salesmen call the son-of-a-gun from head office with the special prices. Need any trucks? How about forty? Give you a real good discount today.

BAIRD [*laughs*]: I couldn't use that many, I'm afraid. Not in my line.

SPENCER: Which is?

BAIRD: Medicine.

SPENCER: You mean you're a doctor?

BAIRD: That's right. Can't buy one truck, leave alone forty. Football is the one extravagance I allow myself.

SPENCER: Delighted to hear it, doctor. Now I can relax. [*As he speaks, the run-up of the aircraft engines begins, increasing* *to a heavy roar.*]

BAIRD [*raising his voice*]: Do you think you can in this racket? I never can figure out why they make all this noise before take-off.

SPENCER [*shouting, as noise increases*]: It's the normal run-up of the engines. Airplane engines don't use battery ignition like you have in your car. They run on magneto ignition, and each of the magnetos is tested separately. If they're okay and the motors are giving all the power they should—away you go!

BAIRD: You sound as if you know something about it.

SPENCER: I'm pretty rusty now. I used to fly fighters in the air force. But that was ten years ago. Reckon I've forgotten most of it. Well, there we go.

> [*The tempo of the motors increases.* BAIRD *and* SPENCER *lean toward the window to watch the take-off, although it is dark outside.*
>
> [CUT TO: *the passenger cabin. The noise of the motor is reduced slightly and the two men relax in their seats.* SPENCER *reaches for cigarettes.*]

SPENCER: Smoke?

BAIRD: Thank you.

> [*They light up.* STEWARDESS *enters from aft of airplane and reaches for two pillows from the rack above.*]

STEWARDESS: We were held up at Winnipeg, sir, and we haven't served dinner yet. Would you care for some?

SPENCER: Yes, please.

> [STEWARDESS *puts a pillow on his lap.*]

STEWARDESS [*to* BAIRD]: And you, sir?

BAIRD: Thank you, yes. [*To* SPENCER.] It's a bit late for dinner, but it'll pass the time away.

STEWARDESS: There's lamb chops or grilled halibut.

BAIRD: I'll take the lamb.

SPENCER: Yes, I'll have that, too.

STEWARDESS: Thank you, sir.

BAIRD [*to* SPENCER]: Tell me . . . By the way, my name is Baird.

SPENCER: Spencer. George Spencer. [*They shake hands.*]

BAIRD: How'd'do. Tell me, when you make a sales trip like this do you . . . .

> [*Fade voices and pan with the* STEWARDESS *returning aft. Entering the airplane's tiny galley she picks up a telephone and presses a call button.*]

VOICE OF THE FIRST OFFICER: Flight deck.

STEWARDESS: I'm finally serving the dinners. What'll "you-all" have—lamb chops or grilled halibut?

VOICE OF THE FIRST OFFICER: Just a minute. [*Pause.*] Skipper says he'll have the lamb . . . Oh, hold it! . . . No, he's changed his mind. Says he'll take the halibut. Make it two fish, Janet.

STEWARDESS: Okay.

> [STEWARDESS *hangs up the phone and begins to arrange meal trays.*
>
> [CUT TO: SPENCER *and* BAIRD.]

SPENCER: No, I hadn't expected to go west again this quickly.

BAIRD: You have my sympathy. I prescribe my travel in small doses. [STEWARDESS *enters and puts meal tray on pillow.*] Oh, thank you.

STEWARDESS: Will you have coffee, tea, or milk, sir?

BAIRD: Coffee, please.

STEWARDESS: I'll bring it later.

BAIRD: That'll be fine. [*To* SPENCER.] Tell me, do you follow football at all?

SPENCER: A little. Hockey's my game, though. Who are you for tomorrow?

BAIRD: The Argos, naturally. [*As the* STEWARDESS *brings second tray.*] Thank you, dear.

STEWARDESS: Will you have coffee, tea or . . . .

SPENCER: I'll have coffee too. No cream. [STEWARDESS *nods and exits. To* BAIRD.] Must be a calm night outside. No trouble in keeping the dinner steady.

BAIRD [*looking out of window*]: It *is* calm. Not a cloud in sight. Must be a monotonous business flying these things once they're off the ground.

SPENCER: It varies, I guess.

[AUDIO: *fade up the roar of motors.*

[DISSOLVE TO: FILM INSERT—*airplane in level flight, night.*

[DISSOLVE TO: *the aircraft flight deck. The* CAPTAIN *is seated on left,* FIRST OFFICER *on right. Neither is touching the controls.*]

FIRST OFFICER [*into radio mike*]: Height 16,000 feet. Course 285 true. ETA Vancouver 0505 Pacific Standard. Over.

RADIO VOICE: Flight 714. This is Winnipeg Control. Roger. Out.

[*The* FIRST OFFICER *reaches for a log sheet and makes a notation, then relaxes in his seat.*]

FIRST OFFICER: Got any plans for Vancouver?

CAPTAIN: Yes, I'm going to sleep for two whole days.

[*The* STEWARDESS *enters with a meal tray.*]

STEWARDESS: Who's first?

CAPTAIN: You take yours, Harry.

[STEWARDESS *produces a pillow and the* FIRST OFFICER *slides back his seat, well clear of control column. He places the pillow on his knees and accepts the tray.*]

FIRST OFFICER: Thanks, honey.

CAPTAIN: Everything all right at the back, Janet? How are the football fans?

STEWARDESS: They tired themselves out on the way from Toronto. Looks like a peaceful, placid night.

FIRST OFFICER [*with mouth full of food, raising fork for emphasis*]: Aha! Those are the sort of nights to beware of. It's in the quiet times that trouble brews. I'll bet you right now that somebody's getting ready to be sick.

STEWARDESS: That'll be when you're doing the flying. Or have you finally learned how to hold this thing steady? [*To* CAPTAIN.] How's the weather?

CAPTAIN: General fog east of the mountains, extending pretty well as far as Manitoba. But it's clear to the west. Should be rockabye smooth the whole way.

STEWARDESS: Good. Well, keep Junior here off the controls while I serve coffee. [*Exits.*]

FIRST OFFICER [*calling after her*]: Mark my words, woman!

Stay close to that mop and pail.

CAPTAIN: How's the fish?

FIRST OFFICER [*hungrily*]: Not bad. Not bad at all. If there were about three times as much, it might be a square meal.

[AUDIO: *fade voices into roar of motors.*

[DISSOLVE TO: *the passenger cabin.* SPENCER *and* BAIRD *are concluding their meal.* BAIRD *puts down a coffee cup and wipes his mouth with a napkin, then he reaches up and presses a call button over his head. There is a soft "ping" and the* STEWARDESS *enters.*]

STEWARDESS: Yes, sir?

BAIRD: That was very enjoyable. Now if you'll take the tray I think I'll try to sleep.

STEWARDESS: Surely. [*To* SPENCER.] Will you have more coffee, sir?

SPENCER: No thanks. [STEWARDESS *picks up the second tray and goes aft.* SPENCER *yawns.*] Let me know if the noise keeps you awake. If it does, I'll have the engines stopped.

BAIRD [*chuckles*]: Well, at least there won't be any night calls— I hope.

[BAIRD *reaches up and switches off the overhead reading lights so that both seats are in semi-darkness. The two men prepare to sleep.*

[DISSOLVE TO: FILM INSERT—*airplane in level flight, night.*

[DISSOLVE TO: *the passenger cabin. The* CAPTAIN *emerges from the flight deck and strolls aft, saying "Good evening" to one or two people who glance up as he goes by. He passes* SPENCER *and* BAIRD, *who are sleeping. As the* CAPTAIN *progresses, the* STEWARDESS *can be seen at the rear of the cabin. She is bending solicitously over a woman passenger, her hand on the woman's forehead. The* CAPTAIN *approaches.*]

CAPTAIN: Something wrong, Miss Burns?

STEWARDESS: This lady is feeling a little unwell. I was going to get her some aspirin. [*To the* WOMAN PASSENGER.] I'll be back in a moment.

CAPTAIN: Sorry to hear that. What seems to be the trouble?

[*The* WOMAN PASSENGER *has her head back and her mouth open. A strand of hair has fallen across her face and she is obviously in pain.*]

FIRST WOMAN PASSENGER [*speaking with effort*]: I'm sorry to be such a nuisance, but it hit me all of a sudden . . . just a few minutes ago . . . dizziness and nausea and a sharp pain . . . [*Indicating abdomen*] down here.

CAPTAIN: Well I think the stewardess will be able to help you.

[STEWARDESS *returns.*]

STEWARDESS: Now, here you are; try these.

[*She hands over two aspirins and a cup of water. The* PASSENGER *takes them, then puts her head back on the seat rest.*]

FIRST WOMAN PASSENGER: Thank you very much. [*She smiles faintly at the* CAPTAIN.]

CAPTAIN [*quietly, taking* STEWARDESS *aside*]: If she gets any worse you'd better let me know and I'll radio ahead. But we've still five hours' flying to the coast. Is there a doctor on board, do you know?

STEWARDESS: There was no one listed as a doctor on the manifest. But I can go around and ask.

CAPTAIN [*looks around*]: Well, most everybody's sleeping now. We'd better not disturb them unless we have to. See how she is in the next half-hour or so. [CAPTAIN *bends down and puts a hand on the woman's shoulder.*] Try to rest, madam, if you can. Miss Burns will take good care of you.

[*The* CAPTAIN *nods to* STEWARDESS *and begins his return to the flight deck. The* STEWARDESS *arranges blanket around the* WOMAN PASSENGER. SPENCER *and* BAIRD *are still sleeping as the* CAPTAIN *passes.*

[DISSOLVE TO: FILM INSERT—*airplane in level flight, night.*

[DISSOLVE TO: *the passenger cabin.* SPENCER *stirs and wakes. Then he glances forward to where the* STEWARDESS *is leaning over another section of seats and her voice can be heard softly.*]

STEWARDESS: I'm sorry to disturb you, but we're trying to find out if there's a doctor on board.

FIRST MALE PASSENGER: Not me, I'm afraid. Is something wrong?

STEWARDESS: One of the passengers is feeling unwell. It's nothing too serious. [*Moving on to the next pair of seats.*] I'm sorry to disturb you, but we're trying to find out if there's a doctor on board.

> [*There is an indistinct answer from the two people just questioned, then* SPENCER *sits forward and calls the* STEWARDESS.]

SPENCER: Stewardess! [*Indicating* BAIRD, *who is still sleeping.*] This gentleman is a doctor.

STEWARDESS: Thank you. I think we'd better wake him. I have two passengers who are quite sick.

SPENCER: All right. [*Shaking* BAIRD*'s arm.*] Doctor! Doctor! Wake up!

BAIRD: Um. Um. what is it?

STEWARDESS: Doctor, I'm sorry to disturb you. But we have two passengers who seem quite sick. I wonder if you'd take a look at them.

BAIRD [*sleepily*]: Yes . . . yes . . . of course.

> [SPENCER *moves out of seat to permit* BAIRD *to reach the aisle.* BAIRD *then follows the* STEWARDESS *aft to the* FIRST WOMAN PASSENGER. *Although a blanket is around her, the woman is shivering and gasping, with her head back and eyes closed. The* DOCTOR *places a hand on her forehead and she opens her eyes.*]

STEWARDESS: This gentleman is a doctor. He's going to help us.

FIRST WOMAN PASSENGER: Oh, Doctor . . . !

BAIRD: Now just relax. [*He makes a quick external examination, first checking pulse, then taking a small pen-type flashlight from his pocket and looking into her eyes. He then loosens the blanket and the* WOMAN'S *coat beneath the blanket. As he places a hand on her abdomen she gasps with* *pain.*] Hurt you there? [*With an effort she nods.*] There?

FIRST WOMAN PASSENGER: Oh yes! Yes!

> [BAIRD *replaces the coat and blanket, then turns to* STEWARDESS.]

BAIRD [*with authority*]: Please tell the Captain we must land at once. This woman has to be gotten to hospital immediately.

STEWARDESS: Do you know what's wrong, Doctor?

BAIRD: I can't tell. I've no means of making a proper diagnosis. But it's serious enough to land at the nearest city with hospital facilities. You can tell your Captain that.

STEWARDESS: Very well, Doctor. [*Moving across the aisle and forward.*] While I'm gone will you take a look at this gentleman here? He's also complained of sickness and stomach pains.

> [BAIRD *goes to a* MALE PASSENGER *indicated by the* STEWARDESS. *The man is sitting forward and resting his head on the back of the seat ahead of him. He is retching.*]

BAIRD: I'm a doctor. Will you put your head back, please? [*The man groans, but follows the doctor's instruction. He is obviously weak.* BAIRD *makes another quick examination, then pauses thoughtfully.*] What have you had to eat in the last 24 hours?

SECOND MALE PASSENGER [*with effort*]: Just the usual meals . . . breakfast . . . bacon and eggs . . . salad for lunch . . . couple of sandwiches at the airport . . . then dinner here.

> [*The* STEWARDESS *enters, followed by the* CAPTAIN.]

BAIRD [*to* STEWARDESS]: Keep him warm. Get blankets around him. [*To* CAPTAIN.] How quickly can we land, Captain?

CAPTAIN: That's the trouble. I've just been talking to Calgary. There was light fog over the prairies earlier, but now it's thickened and everything is closed in this side of the mountains. It's clear at the coast and we'll have to go through.

BAIRD: Is that faster than turning back?

CAPTAIN: It would take us longer to go back now than to go on.

BAIRD: Then how soon do you expect to land?

CAPTAIN: At about five A.M. Pacific time. [*As* BAIRD *glances at his watch.*] You need to put your watch back two hours because of the change of time. We'll be landing in three hours forty-five minutes from now.

BAIRD: Then I'll have to do what I can for these people. Can my bag be reached? I checked it at Toronto.

CAPTAIN: We can get it. Let me have your tags, Doctor.

> [BAIRD *takes out a wallet and selects two baggage tags which he hands to* CAPTAIN.]

BAIRD: There are two bags. It's the small overnight case I want.

> [*As he finishes speaking the airplane lurches violently.* BAIRD *and the* STEWARDESS *and the* CAPTAIN *are thrown sharply to one side. Simultaneously the telephone in the galley buzzes several times. As the three recover their balance the* STEWARDESS *answers the phone quickly.*]

STEWARDESS: Yes?

FIRST OFFICER'S VOICE [*under strain*]: Come forward quickly. I'm sick!

STEWARDESS: The First Officer is sick. He says come quickly.

CAPTAIN [*to* BAIRD]: You'd better come too.

> [*The* CAPTAIN *and* BAIRD *move quickly forward, passing through the flight deck door.*
>
> [CUT TO: *the flight deck. The* FIRST OFFICER *is at the controls on the right-hand side. He is retching and shuddering, flying the airplane by will-power and nothing else. The* CAPTAIN *promptly slides into the left-hand seat and takes the controls.*

CAPTAIN: Get him out of there!

> [*Together* BAIRD *and the* STEWARDESS *lift the* FIRST OFFICER *from his seat and, as they do, he collapses. They lower him to the floor and the* STEWARDESS *reaches for a pillow and blankets.* BAIRD *makes the same quick examination he used in the two previous cases. Meanwhile the* CAPTAIN *has steadied the aircraft and now he snaps over a button to engage the automatic*

*pilot. He releases the controls and turns to the others,
though without leaving his seat.]*

CAPTAIN: He must have been changing course when it happened. We're back on auto pilot now. Now, Doctor, what is it? What's happening?

BAIRD: There's a common denominator in these attacks. There has to be, and the most likely thing is food. [*To* STEWARDESS.] How long is it since we had dinner?

STEWARDESS: Two and a half to three hours.

BAIRD: Now then, what did you serve?

STEWARDESS: Well, the main course was a choice of fish or meat.

BAIRD: I remember that. I ate meat. [*Indicating* FIRST OFFICER.] What did he have?

STEWARDESS [*faintly, with dawning alarm*]: Fish.

BAIRD: Do you remember what the other two passengers had?

STEWARDESS: No.

BAIRD: Then go back quickly and find out, please. [*As the* STEWARDESS *exits* BAIRD *kneels beside* FIRST OFFICER, *who is moaning.*] Try to relax. I'll give you something in a few minutes to help the pain. You'll feel better if you stay warm.

[BAIRD *arranges the blanket around the* FIRST OFFICER. *Now the* STEWARDESS *reappears.*]

STEWARDESS [*alarmed*]: Doctor, both those passengers had fish. And there are three more cases now. And they ate fish too. Can you come?

BAIRD: Yes, but I need that bag of mine.

CAPTAIN: Janet, take these tags and get one of the passengers to help you. [*Hands over* BAIRD'*s luggage tags.*] Doctor, I'm going to get on the radio and report what's happening to Vancouver. Is there anything you want to add?

BAIRD: Yes. Tell them we have three serious cases of suspected food poisoning and there appear to be others. When we land we'll want ambulances and medical help waiting, and the hospitals should be warned. Tell them we're not sure, but we suspect the poisoning may have been caused by fish served on

65

board. You'd better suggest they put a ban on serving all food which originated wherever ours came from until we've established the source for sure.

CAPTAIN: Right. [*He reaches for the radio mike and* BAIRD *turns to go aft. But suddenly a thought strikes the* CAPTAIN.] Doctor, I've just remembered . . . .

BAIRD: Yes.

CAPTAIN [*quietly*]: I ate fish.

BAIRD: When?

CAPTAIN: I'd say about half an hour after he did. [*Pointing to* FIRST OFFICER.] Maybe a little longer. Is there anything I can do?

BAIRD: It doesn't follow that everyone will be affected. There's often no logic to these things. You feel all right now?

CAPTAIN: Yes.

BAIRD: You'd better not take any chances. Your food can't be completely digested yet. As soon as I get my bag I'll give you something to help you get rid of it.

CAPTAIN: Then hurry, Doctor. For God's sake, hurry! [*Into mike.*] Vancouver Control. This is Maple Leaf Charter Flight 714. I have an emergency message. Do you read? Over.

VOICE ON RADIO [VANCOUVER OPERATOR]: Go ahead, 714.

CAPTAIN: We have serious food poisoning on board. Several passengers and the First Officer are seriously ill . . . .

[DISSOLVE TO: *the luggage compartment below the flight deck. A passenger is hurriedly passing up bags to the* STEWARDESS. BAIRD *is looking down from above.*]

BAIRD: That's it! That's it down there! Let me have it!

[FADE OUT]

ACT II

FADE IN: *the Control Room, Vancouver Airport. At a radio panel an* OPERATOR, *wearing headphones, is transcribing a message on a typewriter. Part way through the message he presses a button on the panel and a bell rings stridently, signalling an emergency. At once* *an* AIRPORT CONTROLLER *appears behind the* OPERATOR *and reads the message as it continues to come in. Nearby is a telephone switchboard manned by an operator, and a battery of teletypes clattering noisily.*

CONTROLLER [*over his shoulder, to* SWITCHBOARD OPERATOR]: Get me area traffic control, then clear the teletype circuit to Winnipeg. Priority message. [*Stepping back to take phone.*] Vancouver Controller here. I've an emergency report from Maple Leaf Charter Flight 714, ex-Winnipeg for Vancouver. There's serious food poisoning among the passengers and the First Officer is down too. They're asking for all levels below them to be cleared, and priority approach and landing. ETA is 0505 . . . Roger. We'll keep you posted. [*To a* TELETYPE OPERATOR, *who has appeared.*] Got Winnipeg? [*As* TELETYPE OPERATOR *nods.*] Send this message. Controller Winnipeg. Urgent. Maple Leaf Charter Flight 714 reports serious food poisoning among passengers believed due to fish dinner served on flight. Imperative check source and suspend all other food service originating same place. That's all. [*To* SWITCHBOARD OPERATOR.] Get me the local agent for Maple Leaf Charter. Burdick's his name—call his home. And after that I want the city police—the senior officer on duty. [CONTROLLER *crosses to radio control panel and reads message which is just being completed. To* RADIO OPERATOR.] Acknowledge. Say that all altitudes below them are being cleared and they'll be advised of landing instructions here. Ask them to keep us posted on condition of the passengers.

SWITCHBOARD OPERATOR: Mr. Burdick is here at the airport. I have him on the line now.

CONTROLLER: Good. Controller here. Burdick, we've got an emergency message on one of your fights—714, ex-Toronto and Winnipeg. [*Pause.*] No, the aircraft is all right. There's food poisoning among the passengers and the First Officer has it too. You'd better come over. [*Replaces phone. Then to* SWITCHBOARD OPERATOR.] Have you got the police yet? [*As* OPERATOR *nods.*] Right, put it on this line. Hullo, this is the Controller, Vancouver

Airport. Who am I speaking to, please? [*Pause.*] Inspector, we have an emergency on an incoming flight. Several of the passengers are seriously ill and we need ambulances and doctors out here at the airport. [*Pause.*] Six people for sure, maybe more. The flight will be landing at five minutes past five local time—that's in about three and a half hours. Now, will you get the ambulances, set up traffic control and alert the hospitals? Right. We'll call you again as soon as there's anything definite.

> [*During the above,* HARRY BURDICK, *local manager of Maple Leaf Air Charter, has entered.*]

BURDICK: Where's the message? [RADIO OPERATOR *hands him a copy, which* BURDICK *reads.*] How's the weather at Calgary? It might be quicker to go in there.

CONTROLLER: No dice! There's fog down to the deck everywhere east of the Rockies. They'll have to come through.

BURDICK: Let me see the last position report. [*As* CONTROLLER *passes a clipboard.*] You say you've got medical help coming?

CONTROLLER: The city police are working on it now.

BURDICK: That message! They say the First Officer is down. What about the Captain? Ask if he's affected, and ask if there's a doctor on board. Tell them we're getting medical advice here in case they need it.

CONTROLLER: I'll take care of that.

BURDICK [*to* SWITCHBOARD OPERATOR]: Will you get me Doctor Knudsen, please. You'll find his home number on the emergency list.

CONTROLLER [*into radio mike*]: Flight 714, this is Vancouver.

> [DISSOLVE TO: *the airplane passenger cabin.* BAIRD *is leaning over another prostrate passenger. The main lighting is on in the cabin and other passengers, so far not affected, are watching with varying degrees of concern and anxiety. Some have remained in their seats, others have clustered in the aisle. The* DOCTOR *has obtained his bag and it is open beside him. The* STEWARDESS *is attending to another passenger nearby.*]

BAIRD [*to* STEWARDESS]: I think I'd better talk to everyone and tell them the story. [*Moving to center of cabin, he raises his voice.*] Ladies and gentlemen, may I have your attention, please? If you can't hear me, perhaps you would come a little closer. [*Pause, as passengers move in.*] My name is Baird and I am a doctor. I think it's time that everyone knew what is happening. So far as I can tell, we have several cases of food poisoning and we believe that the cause of it was the fish which was served for dinner.

SECOND WOMAN PASSENGER [*with alarm, to man beside her*]: Hector! We both had fish!

BAIRD: Now, there is no immediate cause for alarm or panic, and even if you did eat fish for dinner, it doesn't follow that you are going to be affected too. There's seldom any logic to these things. However, we are going to take some precautions and the stewardess and I are coming around to everyone, and I want you to tell us if you ate fish. If you did we'll tell you what to do to help yourselves. Now, if you'll go back to your seats we'll begin right away. [*To* STEWARDESS, *as passengers move back to their seats.*] All we can do now is to give immediate first aid.

STEWARDESS: What should that be, Doctor?

BAIRD: Two things. First, everyone who ate fish must drink several glasses of water. That will help to dilute the poison. After that we'll give an emetic. I have some emetic pills in my bag, and if there aren't enough we'll have to rely on salt. Do you have salt in the galley?

STEWARDESS: A few small packets which go with the lunches, but we can break them open.

BAIRD: All right. We'll see how far the pills will go first. I'll start at the back here. Meanwhile you begin giving drinking water to the passengers already affected and get some to the First Officer too. I'll ask someone to help you.

FIRST MALE PASSENGER: Can I help, Doctor?

BAIRD: What did you eat for dinner—fish or meat?

FIRST MALE PASSENGER: Meat.

BAIRD: All right. Will you help the stewardess bring glasses of water to the people who are sick? I want them to drink at least three glasses each—more if they can.

STEWARDESS [*going to galley*]: We'll use these cups. There's drinking water here and at the rear.

FIRST MALE PASSENGER: All right, let's get started.

BAIRD [*to* STEWARDESS]: The Captain! Before you do anything else you'd better get him on to drinking water, and give him two emetic pills. Here. [*Takes bottle from his bag and shakes out the pills.*] Tell him they'll make him feel sick, and the sooner he is, the better.

STEWARDESS: Very well, Doctor.

SECOND WOMAN PASSENGER [*frightened*]: Doctor! Doctor! I heard you say the pilots are ill. What will happen to us if they can't fly the plane? Hector, I'm frightened.

THIRD MALE PASSENGER: Take it easy, my dear. Nothing has happened so far and the doctor is doing all he can.

BAIRD: I don't think you'll have any reason to worry, madam. It's quite true that both of the pilots had the fish which we believe may have caused the trouble. But only the First Officer is affected. Now, did you and your husband eat fish or meat?

THIRD MALE PASSENGER: Fish. We both ate fish.

BAIRD: Then will you both drink at least—better make it four—of those cups of water which the other gentleman is bringing around. After that, take one of these pills each. [*Smiling.*] I think you'll find there are little containers under your seat. Use those. [*Goes to rear of plane.*]

FOURTH MALE PASSENGER [*in broad English Yorkshire accent*]: How's it comin', Doc? Everything under control?

BAIRD: I think we're holding our own. What did you have for dinner?

FOURTH MALE PASSENGER: Ah had the bloomin' fish. Didn't like it neither. Fine how-d'you-do this is. Coom all this way t'see our team win, and now it looks like Ah'm headed for a mortuary slab.

BAIRD: It really isn't as bad as that, you know. But just as a precaution, drink four cups of water—it's being brought around now—and after that take this pill. It'll make you feel sick.

FOURTH MALE PASSENGER [*pulling carton from under seat and holding it up*]: It's the last time I ride on a bloomin' airplane! What a service! They give you your dinner and then coom round and ask for it back.

BAIRD: What did you have for dinner, please—meat or fish?

SECOND MALE PASSENGER: Meat, Doctor.

FIFTH MALE PASSENGER: Yes, I had meat too.

BAIRD: All right, we won't worry about you.

SIXTH MALE PASSENGER: I had meat, Doctor.

SEVENTH MALE PASSENGER: I had fish.

BAIRD: Very well. Will you drink at least four cups of water, please? It'll be brought round to you. Then take this pill.

SIXTH MALE PASSENGER [*slow-speaking; a little dull-witted*]: What's caused this food poisoning, Doctor?

BAIRD: Well, it can either be caused through spoilage of the food, or some kind of bacteria—the medical word is staphylococcus poisoning.

SIXTH MALE PASSENGER [*nodding knowledgeably*]: Oh, yes . . . staphylo . . . I see.

BAIRD: Either that, or some toxic substance may have gotten into the food during its preparation.

SEVENTH MALE PASSENGER: Which kind do you think this is, doctor?

BAIRD: From the effect I suspect a toxic substance.

SEVENTH MALE PASSENGER: And you don't know what it is?

BAIRD: We won't know until we make laboratory tests. Actually, with modern food-handling methods—the chances of this happening are probably a million to one against.

STEWARDESS [*entering*]: I couldn't get the First Officer to take more than a little water, Doctor. He seems pretty bad.

BAIRD: I'll go to him now. Have you checked all the passengers in the front portion?

STEWARDESS: Yes, and there are two more new cases—the same symptoms as the others.

BAIRD: I'll attend to them—after I've looked at the First Officer.

STEWARDESS: Do you think....

[*Before the sentence is completed the galley telephone buzzes insistently.* BAIRD *and the* STEWARDESS *exchange glances quickly, then, without waiting to answer the phone, race to the flight deck door.*

[CUT TO: *the flight deck. The* CAPTAIN *is in the left-hand seat. Sweat pouring down his face, he is racked by retching and his right hand is on his stomach. Yet he is fighting against the pain and attempting to reach the radio transmitter mike. But he doesn't make it and, as* BAIRD *and the* STEWARDESS *reach him, he falls back in his seat.*]

CAPTAIN [*weakly*]: I did what you said ... guess it was too late ...You've got to give me something, Doctor ... so I can hold out ... till I see this airplane on the ground ...You understand?... It'll fly itself on this course ... but I've got to take it in ... Get on the radio ...Tell control....

[*During the above* BAIRD *and the* STEWARDESS *have been helping the* CAPTAIN *from his seat. Now he collapses into unconsciousness and* BAIRD *goes down beside him. The* DOCTOR *has a stethoscope now and uses it, then makes the other checks quickly and efficiently.*]

BAIRD: Get blankets over him. Keep him warm. There's probably a reaction because he tried to fight it off so long.

STEWARDESS [*alarmed*]: Can you do what he said? Can you bring him round long enough to land?

BAIRD [*bluntly*]: You're part of this crew, so I'll tell you how things are. Unless I can get him to a hospital quickly I'm not even sure I can save his life. And that goes for the others too.

STEWARDESS: But ....

BAIRD: I know what you're thinking, and I've thought of it too. How many passengers are there on board?

STEWARDESS: Fifty-six.

BAIRD: And how many fish dinners did you serve?

STEWARDESS [*composing herself*]: Probably about 15. More people ate meat than fish, and some didn't eat at all because it

72

was so late.

BAIRD: And you?

STEWARDESS: I had meat.

BAIRD [*quietly*]: My dear, did you ever hear the term "long odds"?

STEWARDESS: Yes, but I'm not sure what it means.

BAIRD: I'll give you an example. Out of a total field of 55, our chance of safety depends on there being one person back there who not only is qualified to land this airplane, but who didn't choose fish for dinner tonight.

> [*After her initial alarm the* STEWARDESS *is calm now, and competent. She looks* BAIRD *in the eye and even manages a slight smile.*]

STEWARDESS: Then I suppose I should begin asking.

BAIRD [*thoughtfully*]: Yes, but there's no sense in starting a panic. [*Decisively.*] You'd better do it this way. Say that the First Officer is sick and the Captain wondered if there's someone with flying experience who could help him with the radio.

STEWARDESS: Very well, Doctor. [*She turns to go.*]

BAIRD: Wait! The man who was sitting beside me! He said something about flying in the war. And we both ate meat. Get him first! But still go round the others. There may be someone else with more experience.

> [STEWARDESS *exits and* BAIRD *busies himself with the* FIRST OFFICER *and the* CAPTAIN. *After a moment,* GEORGE SPENCER *enters.*]

SPENCER: The Stewardess said . . . [*Then, as he sees the two pilots.*] No! Not both pilots!

BAIRD: Can you fly this airplane—and land it?

SPENCER: No! No! Not a chance! Of course not!

BAIRD: But you told me you flew in the war.

SPENCER: So I did. But that was fighters—little combat airplanes, not a great ship like this. I flew airplanes which had one engine. This has four. Flying characteristics are different. Controls don't react the same way. It's another kind of flying altogether. And besides that, I haven't touched an airplane for over ten years.

BAIRD [*grimly*]: Then let's hope there's someone else on board who can do the job...because neither of these men can.

[STEWARDESS *enters and pauses*.]

STEWARDESS [*quietly*]: There's no one else.

BAIRD: Mr. Spencer, I know nothing of flying. I have no means of evaluating what you tell me. All I know is this: that among the people on this airplane who are physically able to fly it, you are the only one with any kind of qualifications to do so. What do you suggest?

SPENCER [*desperately*]: Isn't there a chance—of either pilot recovering?

BAIRD: I'll tell you what I just told the stewardess here. Unless I can get them to hospital quickly, I can't even be sure of saving their lives. [*There is a pause.*]

SPENCER: Well—I guess I just got drafted. If either of you are any good at praying, you can start any time. [*He slips into the left-hand seat.*] Let's take a look. Altitude 16,000. Course 290. The ship's on automatic pilot—we can be thankful for that. Air speed 210 knots. [*Touching the various controls.*] Throttles, pitch, mixture, landing gear, flaps, and the flap indicator. We'll need a check list for landing, but we'll get that on the radio ... Well, maybe we'd better tell the world about our problems. [*To* STEWARDESS.] Do you know how to work this radio? They've added a lot of gizmos since my flying days.

STEWARDESS [*pointing*]: It's this panel up here they use to talk to the ground, but I'm not sure which switches you have to set.

SPENCER: Ah yes, here's the channel selector. Maybe we'd better leave it where it is. Oh, and here we are—"transmit." [*He flicks a switch and a small light glows on the radio control panel.*] Now we're in business. [*He picks up the mike and headset beside him, then turns to the other two.*] Look, whatever happens I'm going to need another pair of hands here. Doc, I guess you'll be needed back with the others, so I think the best choice is Miss Canada here. How about it?

STEWARDESS: But I know nothing about all this!

SPENCER: Then that'll make us a real good pair. But I'll tell you

74

what to do ahead of time. Better get in that other seat and strap yourself in. That all right with you, Doc?

BAIRD: Yes, do that. I'll take care of things in the back. And I'd better go there now. Good luck!

SPENCER: Good luck to *you*. We're all going to need it.

[BAIRD *exits*.]

SPENCER: What's your first name?

STEWARDESS: Janet.

SPENCER: Okay, Janet. Let's see if I can remember how to send out a distress message . . . Better put on that headset beside you. [*Into mike*.] Mayday! Mayday! Mayday! [*To* STEWARDESS.] What's our flight number?

STEWARDESS: 714.

SPENCER [*into mike*]: This is Flight 714, Maple Leaf Air Charter, in distress. Come in anyone. Over.

VOICE ON RADIO [*immediately, crisply*]: This is Calgary, 714. Go ahead!

VOICE ON RADIO [VANCOUVER OPERATOR]: Vancouver here, 714. All other aircraft stay off the air. Over.

SPENCER: Thank you, Calgary and Vancouver. This message is for Vancouver. This aircraft is in distress. Both pilots and some passengers . . . [*To* STEWARDESS.] How many passengers?

STEWARDESS: It was seven a few minutes ago. It may be more now.

SPENCER: Correction. At least seven passengers are suffering from food poisoning. Both pilots are unconscious and in serious condition. We have a doctor on board who says that neither pilot can be revived. Did you get that, Vancouver? [*Pause*.] Now we come to the interesting bit. My name is Spencer, George Spencer. I am a passenger on this airplane. Correction: I *was* a passenger. I have about a thousand hours' total flying time, but all of it was on single-engine fighters. And also I haven't flown an airplane for ten years. Now then, Vancouver, you'd better get someone on this radio who can give me some instructions about flying this machine. Our altitude is 16,000, course 290 magnetic, air speed 210 knots. We are on automatic pilot. Your

75

move, Vancouver. Over. [*To* STEWARDESS.] You want to take a bet that that stirred up a little flurry down below?

> [*The* STEWARDESS *shakes her head, but does not reply.*
> [DISSOLVE TO: *the Control Room, Vancouver. The* CONTROLLER *is putting down a phone as the* RADIO OPERATOR *brings a message to him. He reads the message.*]

CONTROLLER: Oh, no! [*To* RADIO OPERATOR.] Ask if . . . No, let me talk to them. [*Goes to panel and takes the transmitter mike. The* RADIO OPERATOR *turns a switch and nods. Tensely.*] Flight 714. This is Vancouver Control. Please check with your doctor on board for any possibility of either pilot recovering. Ask him to do everything possible to revive one of the pilots, even if it means neglecting other people. Over.

SPENCER'S VOICE ON RADIO: Vancouver, this is 714, Spencer speaking. I understand your message. But the doctor says there is no possibility whatever of either pilot recovering to make the landing. He says they are critically ill and may die unless they get hospital treatment soon. Over.

CONTROLLER: All right, 714. Stand by, please. [*He pauses momentarily to consider the next course of action. Then briskly to* SWITCHBOARD OPERATOR.] Get me area traffic control— fast. [*Into phone.*] Vancouver Controller. The emergency we had—right now it looks like it's shaping up for a disaster.

> [FADE OUT]

ACT III

> **FADE IN:** *the Control Room, Vancouver. The atmosphere is one of restrained pandemonium. The* RADIO OPERATOR *is typing a message. The teletypes are busy. The* CONTROLLER *is on one telephone and* HARRY BURDICK *on another. During what follows cut back and forth from one to the other.*

CONTROLLER [*into phone*]: As of right now, hold everything taking off for the east. You've got 45 minutes to clear any traffic for south, west, or north. After that, hold everything that's scheduled outwards. On incoming traffic, accept anything you can get on the deck within the next 45 minutes. Anything you can't get down by then for sure, divert away from this area. Hold it. [*A* MESSENGER *hands him a message, which he scans. Then to* MESSENGER.] Tell the security officer. [*Into phone*.] If you've any flights coming in from the Pacific, divert them to Seattle. And any traffic inland is to stay well away from the east-west lane between Calgary and Vancouver. Got that? Right.

BURDICK [*into phone*]: Is that Cross-Canada Airlines? . . . Who's on duty in operations? . . . Let me talk to him. [*Pause.*] Mr. Gardner, it's Harry Burdick of Maple Leaf Charter. We have an incoming flight that's in bad trouble and we need an experienced pilot to talk on the radio. Someone who's flown DC-4's. Can you help us? [*Pause.*] Captain Treleaven? Yes, I know him well. [*Pause.*] You mean he's with you now? [*Pause.*] Thank you. Thank you very much. [*To* SWITCHBOARD OPERATOR.] Get me Montreal. I want to talk with Mr. Barney Whitmore. You may have to try the Maple Leaf Air Charter office first, and someone there'll have his home number. Tell them the call is urgent.

SWITCHBOARD OPERATOR: Right. [*To* CONTROLLER.] I've got the fire chief.

CONTROLLER [*into phone*]: Chief, we have an emergency. It's Flight 714, due here at 0505. It may be a crash landing. Have everything you've got stand by. If you have men off duty call them in. Take your instructions from the Tower. They'll tell you which runway we're using. And notify the city fire department. They may want to move equipment into this area. Tight. [*To* SWITCHBOARD OPERATOR.] Now get me the city police again—Inspector Moyse.

SWITCHBOARD OPERATOR: I have Seattle and Calgary waiting. They both received the message from flight 714 and want to know if we got it clearly.

CONTROLLER: Tell them thank you, yes, and we're working the aircraft direct. But ask them to keep a listening watch in case we run into any reception trouble. [*Another message is handed him. After reading, he passes it to* BURDICK.] There's bad weather moving in. That's all we need. [*To* SWITCHBOARD OPERATOR.] Have you got the police? Right! [*Into phone.*] It's the airport controller again, Inspector. We're in bad trouble and we may have a crash landing. We'll need every spare ambulance in the city out here—and doctors and nurses too. Will you arrange it? [*Pause.*] Yes, we do—56 passengers and a crew of three. [*Pause.*] Yes, the same time—0505. That's less than three hours.

BURDICK [*to* SWITCHBOARD]: Is Montreal on the line yet? Yes, give it to me. Hullo. Hullo. Is that you, Barney? It's Harry Burdick in Vancouver. I'll give you this fast, Barney. Our flight from Toronto is in bad trouble. They have food poisoning on board and both pilots and a lot of the passengers have passed out. There's a doctor on board and he says there's no chance of recovery before they get to hospital. [*Pause.*] No, he isn't qualified. He flew single-engine fighters in the war, nothing since. [*Pause.*] I've asked him that. This doctor on board says there isn't a chance. [*Pause.*] What else can we do? We've got to talk him down. Cross-Canada are lending us a pilot. It's Captain Treleaven, one of their senior men. He's here now, just arrived. We'll get on the radio with a checklist and try to bring him in. [*Pause.*] We'll do the best we can. [*Pause. Then impatiently.*] Of course it's a terrible risk, but can you think of something better? [*Pause.*] No, the papers aren't on to it yet, but don't worry, they will be soon. We can't help that now. [*Pause. Anxious to get off phone.*] That's all we know, Barney. It only just happened, I called you right away. ETA is 0505 Pacific time; that's just under two hours. I've got a lot to do, Barney. I'll have to get on with it. [*Pause. Nodding impatiently.*] I'll call you. I'll call you as soon as I know anything more . . . G'bye. [*During the foregoing* CAPTAIN MARTIN TRELEAVEN, *45, has entered. He is wearing airline uniform. As* BURDICK *sees* TRELEAVEN, *he beckons him, indicating that he should listen. To* TRELEAVEN.] Did you get that?

TRELEAVEN [*calmly*]: Is that the whole story?

BURDICK: That's everything we know. Now what I want you to do is get on the horn and talk this pilot down. You'll have to help him get the feel of the airplane on the way. You'll have to talk him round the circuit. You'll have to give him the cockpit check for landing, and—so help me!—you'll have to talk him on to the ground.

[CAPTAIN TRELEAVEN *is a calm man, not easily perturbed. While* BURDICK *has been talking, the* CAPTAIN *has been filling his pipe. Now, with methodical movements, he puts away his tobacco pouch and begins to light the pipe.*]

TRELEAVEN [*quietly*]: You realize, of course, that the chances of a man who has only flown fighter airplanes landing a four-engine passenger ship safely are about nine to one against.

BURDICK [*rattled*]: Of course I know it! You heard what I told Whitmore. But do you have any other ideas?

TRELEAVEN: No. I just wanted to be sure you knew what we are getting into, Harry. All right. Let's get started. Where do I go?

CONTROLLER: Over here.

[*They cross to the radio panel and the* OPERATOR *hands him the last message from the aircraft. When he has read it he takes the transmitter mike.*]

TRELEAVEN: How does this thing work?

RADIO OPERATOR [*turning a switch*]: You're on the air now.

TRELEAVEN [*calmly*]: Hullo, Flight 714. This is Vancouver and my name is Martin Treleaven. I am a Cross-Canada Airlines captain and my job right now is to help fly this airplane in. First of all, are you hearing me okay? Over.

VOICE OF SPENCER: Yes, Captain, loud and clear. Go ahead, please.

TRELEAVEN: Where's the message? [*As* OPERATOR *passes it, into mike.*] I see that I'm talking to George Spencer. Well, George, I don't think you're going to have much trouble. These DC-4s handle easily, and we'll give you the drill for landing. But first of all, please tell me what your flying experience is. The message says you have flown single-engine fighters. What kind of airplanes were they, and did you fly multi-engine airplanes at all? Let's hear from you, George. Over.

[CUT TO: *the flight deck.*]

SPENCER [*into mike*]: Hullo, Vancouver, this is 714. Glad to have you along, Captain. But let's not kid each other, please. We both know we need a lot of luck. About my flying. It was mostly on Spitfires and Mustangs. And I have around a thousand hours total. And all that was ten years ago. Over.

[CUT TO: *the Control Room.*]

TRELEAVEN [*into mike*]: Don't worry about that, George. It's like riding a bicycle. You never forget it. Stand by.

CONTROLLER [*to* TRELEAVEN]: The air force has picked up the airplane on radar and they'll be giving us courses to bring him in. [*Hands over paper.*] Here's the first one. See if you can get him on that heading.

TRELEAVEN [*nods; then into mike*]: 714, are you still on automatic pilot? If so, look for the auto-pilot release switch. It's a pushbutton on the control yoke and is plainly marked. Over.

[CUT TO: *the flight deck.*]

SPENCER [*into mike*]: Yes, Vancouver. I see the auto-pilot switch. Over.

[CUT TO: *the Control Room.*]

TRELEAVEN [*into mike*]: Now, George, in a minute you can unlock the automatic pilot and get the feel of the controls, and we're going to change your course a little. But first listen carefully. When you use the controls they will seem very heavy and sluggish compared with a fighter airplane. But don't worry, that's quite normal. You must take care, though, to watch your air speed carefully and do not let it fall below 120 knots while your wheels and flaps are up. Otherwise you will stall. Now, do you have someone up there who can work the radio to leave you free for flying? Over.

[cut to: *the flight deck.*]

SPENCER [*into mike*]: Yes, Vancouver. I have the stewardess here with me and she will take over the radio now. I am going to unlock the automatic pilot. Over. [*To* STEWARDESS *as he depresses the auto-pilot release.*] Well, here we go.

[*Feeling the controls,* SPENCER *eases into a left turn. Then, straightening out, he eases the control column slightly forward and back.*

[CUT TO: *the Control Room.*]

TRELEAVEN'S VOICE: Hullo, 714. How are you making out, George? Have you got the feel of her yet?

[CUT TO: *the flight deck.*]

SPENCER: Tell him I'm on manual now and trying out some gentle turns.

STEWARDESS [*into mike*]**:** Hullo, Vancouver. We are on manual now and trying out some gentle turns.

[CUT TO: *the Control Room*]

TRELEAVEN [*into mike*]**:** Hullo, George Spencer. Try the effect of fore-and-aft control on your air speed. To begin with, close your throttles slightly and bring your air speed back to 160. Adjust the trim as you go along. But watch that air speed closely. Remember to keep it well above 120. Over.

[CUT TO: *the flight deck.*]

SPENCER [*tensely. Still feeling out the controls*]**:** Tell him okay.

STEWARDESS [*into mike*]**:** Okay, Vancouver. We are doing as you say.

TRELEAVEN'S VOICE [*after a pause*]**:** Hullo, 714. How does she handle, George?

SPENCER [*disgustedly*]**:** Tell him sluggish like a wet sponge.

STEWARDESS: Sluggish like a wet sponge, Vancouver.

[CUT TO: *the Control Room. There is a momentary relaxing of tension as* CAPTAIN TRELEAVEN *and the group around him exchange grins.*]

TRELEAVEN [*into mike*]**:** Hullo, George Spencer. That would be a natural feeling because you were used to handling smaller airplanes. The thing you have got to remember is that there is a bigger lag in the effect of control movements on air speed, compared with what you were used to before. Do you understand that? Over.

[CUT TO: *the flight deck.*]

SPENCER: Tell him I understand.

STEWARDESS [*into mike*]**:** Hullo, Vancouver. Yes, he understands. Over.

81

[CUT TO: *the Control Room.*]

TRELEAVEN [*into mike*]: Hullo, George Spencer. Because of that lag in air speed you must avoid any violent movements of the controls, such as you used to make in your fighter airplanes. If you *do* move the controls violently, you will over-correct and be in trouble. Is that understood? Over.

[CUT TO: *the flight deck.*]

SPENCER [*nodding, beginning to perspire*]: Tell him—yes, I understand.

STEWARDESS [*into mike*]: Yes, Vancouver. Your message is understood. Over.

[CUT TO: *the Control Room.*]

TRELEAVEN [*into mike*]: Hullo, George Spencer. Now I want you to feel how the ship handles at lower speeds when the flaps and wheels are down. But don't do anything until I give you the instructions. Is that clear? Over.

[CUT TO: *the flight deck.*]

SPENCER: Tell him okay: let's have the instructions.

STEWARDESS [*into mike*]: Hullo, Vancouver. Yes, we understand. Go ahead with the instructions. Over.

TRELEAVEN'S VOICE: First of all, throttle back slightly, get your air speed steady at 160 knots, and adjust your trim to maintain level flight. Then tell me when you're ready. Over.

SPENCER: Watch that air speed, Janet. You'll have to call it off to me when we land, so you may as well start practicing.

STEWARDESS: It's 200 now . . . 190 . . . 185 . . . 180 . . . 175 . . . 175 . . . 165 . . . 155 . . . 150 . . . [*Alarmed*] That's too low! He said 160!

SPENCER [*tensely*]: I know. I know. Watch it! It's that lag on the air speed I can't get used to.

STEWARDESS: . . . 150 . . . 150 . . . 155 . . . 160 . . . 160 . . . It's steady on 160.

SPENCER: Tell them.

STEWARDESS [*into mike*]: Hullo, Vancouver. This is 714. Our speed is steady at 160. Over.

[CUT TO: *the Control Room.*]

TRELEAVEN [*into mike*]: Okay, 714. Now, George, I want you

82

to put down 20 degrees of flap. But be careful not to make it any more. The flap lever is at the base of the control pedestal and is plainly marked. Twenty degrees will mean moving the lever down to the second notch. Over.

[CUT TO: *the flight deck.*]

SPENCER: Janet, you'll have to put the flaps down. [*Pointing.*] There's the lever.

TRELEAVEN'S VOICE: Can you see the flap indicator, George? It's near the center of the main panel.

SPENCER: Here's the indicator he's talking about. When I tell you, push the lever down to the second notch and watch the dial. Okay?

STEWARDESS: Okay. [*Then with alarm.*] Oh, look at the air speed! It's down to 125!

[SPENCER *grimaces and pushes the control column forward.*]

SPENCER [*urgently*]: Call off the speed! Call off the speed!

STEWARDESS: 140 . . . 150 . . . 160 . . . 170 . . . 175 . . . Can't you get back to 160?

SPENCER [*straining*]: I'm trying! I'm trying! [*Pause.*] There it is.

[CUT TO: *the passenger cabin.*]

SECOND WOMAN PASSENGER [*frightened*]: Hector! Hector! We're going to crash! I know it! Oh, do something! Do something!

BAIRD [*he appears at her elbow*]: Have her take this. It'll help calm her down. [*Gives pill and cup to* THIRD MALE PASSENGER.] Try not to worry. That young man at the front is a very experienced pilot. He's just what they call "getting the feel" of the airplane. [*He moves aft in the cabin.*]

FIRST MALE PASSENGER: Doctor!

BAIRD: Yes.

FIRST MALE PASSENGER: Tell us the truth, Doctor. Have we got a chance? Does this fellow know how to fly this thing?

BAIRD: We've got all kinds of chances. He's a very experienced pilot, but it's just that he's not used to flying this particular type and he's getting the feel of it.

FOURTH MALE PASSENGER: You didn't need none of them pills to make me sick. Never mind me dinner. Now Ah'm worried about yesterday's breakfast.

[CUT TO: *the flight deck.*]

STEWARDESS [*into mike*]: Hullo, Vancouver. Air speed is 160 and we are ready to put down the flaps. Over.

[CUT TO: *the Control Room.*]

TRELEAVEN [*into mike*]: Okay, 714. Go ahead with your flaps. But be careful—only 20 degrees. Then, when you have 20 degrees down, bring back the air speed to 140, adjust your trim, and call me again. Over.

[CUT TO to: *the flight deck.*]

SPENCER: Okay, Janet—flaps down! 20 degrees. [*The* STEWARDESS *pushes down the flap lever to its second notch.*] Tell them we've got the flaps down, and the air speed's coming to 140.

STEWARDESS [*into mike*]: Hullo, Vancouver. This is 714. The flaps are down and our air speed is 140.

[CUT TO: *the Control Room.*]

TRELEAVEN: All right, 714. Now the next thing is to put the wheels down. Are you still maintaining level flight?

[CUT TO: *the flight deck.*]

SPENCER: Tell him—more or less.

STEWARDESS [*into mike*]: Hullo, Vancouver. More or less.

[CUT TO: *the Control Room.*]

RADIO OPERATOR: This guy's got a sense of humor.

BURDICK: That's a real help.

TRELEAVEN [*into mike*]: Okay, 714. Try to keep your altitude steady and your speed at 140. Then when you *are* ready, put down the landing gear and let your speed come back to 120. You will have to advance your throttle setting to maintain that air speed, and also adjust your trim. Is that understood? Over.

[CUT TO: *the flight deck.*]

SPENCER: Ask him—what about the propeller controls and mixture?

STEWARDESS [*into mike*]: Hullo, Vancouver. What about the propeller controls and mixture? Over.

[CUT TO: *the Control Room.*]

CONTROLLER: He's thinking, anyway.

TRELEAVEN [*into mike*]: Leave them alone for the time being. Just concentrate on holding that air speed steady with the wheels and flaps down. Over.

[CUT TO: *the flight deck.*]

SPENCER: Wheels down, Janet, and call off the air speed.

STEWARDESS [*puts landing gear down*]: 140...145...140...135 ...130...125...120...115...The speed's too low!

SPENCER: Keep calling it!!

STEWARDESS: 115...120...120...Steady on 120.

[CUT TO: *the Control Room.*]

TRELEAVEN [*into mike*]: Hullo, George Spencer. Your wheels should be down by now and look for three green lights to show that they're locked. Over.

[CUT TO: *the flight deck.*]

SPENCER: Are they on?

STEWARDESS: Yes—all three lights are green.

SPENCER: Tell them.

STEWARDESS [*into mike*]: Hullo, Vancouver. Yes, there are three green lights.

[CUT TO: *the Control Room.*]

TRELEAVEN: Okay, 714, now let's put down full flap so that you can feel how the airplane will handle when you're landing. As soon as full flap is down, bring your air speed back to 110 knots and trim to hold it steady. Adjust your throttle setting to hold your altitude. Is that understood? Over.

[CUT TO: *the flight deck.*]

SPENCER: Tell him "yes."

STEWARDESS [*into mike*]: Yes, Vancouver. That is understood.

SPENCER: Full flap, Janet! Push the lever all the way down, and call off the air speed.

STEWARDESS: 120...115...115...110...110....

SPENCER: Okay, tell 'em we've got full flap and air speed 110, and she still handles like a sponge, only more so.

STEWARDESS [*into mike*]: Hullo, Vancouver. We have full flap,

85

and air speed is 110. And the pilot says she still handles like a sponge, only more so.

> [CUT TO: *the Control room. Again there is a momentary sense of relief.*]

TRELEAVEN [*into mike*]: That's nice going, George. Now I'm going to give you instructions for holding your height and air speed while you raise the flaps and landing gear. Then we'll run through the whole procedure again.

> [CUT TO: *the flight deck.*]

SPENCER: Again! I don't know if my nerves'll stand it. [*Pause.*] All right. Tell him okay.

> [DISSOLVE TO: *Control Room clock showing 2:55.*
>
> [DISSOLVE TO: *Control Room clock showing 5:20.*
>
> [DISSOLVE TO: *the Control Room.* CAPTAIN TRELEAVEN *is still seated in front of the transmitter, but has obviously been under strain. He now has his coat off and his tie loosened and there is an empty carton of coffee beside him.* BURDICK *and the* CONTROLLER *are in background, watching tensely. A phone rings and the* CONTROLLER *answers it. He makes a note and passes it to* TRELEAVEN.]

TRELEAVEN [*into mike*]: Hullo, Flight 714. Our flying practice has slowed you down and you are later than we expected. You are now 12 minutes' flying time from Vancouver Airport, but it's getting light, so your landing will be in daylight. You should be able to see us at any minute. Do you see the airport beacon? Over.

STEWARDESS'S VOICE: Yes, we see the airport beacon. Over.

TRELEAVEN: Okay George, now you've practiced everything we need for a landing. You've flown the ship with wheels and flaps down, and you know how she handles. Your fuel feeds are checked and you're all set to come in. You won't hear from me again for a few minutes because I'm moving to the Control Tower so I'll be able to see you on the circuit and approach. Is that clear? Over.

STEWARDESS'S VOICE: Yes, Vancouver, that is understood. Over.

TRELEAVEN: All right, George. Continue to approach at two thousand feet on your present heading and wait for instructions. We'll let you know the runway to use at the last minute because the wind is shifting. Don't forget we want you to do at least one dummy run, and then go round again so you'll have practice in making the landing approach. Over. [*He mops his forehead with a crumpled handkerchief.*]

[CUT TO: *the flight deck.* SPENCER, *too, has his coat off and tie loosened. His hair is ruffled and the strain is plainly beginning to tell on him. The* STEWARDESS *is still in the co-pilot's seat and* BAIRD *is standing behind them both. The* STEWARDESS *is about to acknowledge the last radio message, but* SPENCER *stops her.*]

SPENCER: I'll take it, Janet. [*Into mike.*] No dice, Vancouver. We're coming straight in and the first time is "it." Dr. Baird is here beside me. He reports two of the passengers and the First Officer are in critical condition, and we must land in the next few minutes. The doctor asks that you have stomach pumps and oxygen equipment ready. Over.

[CUT TO: *the Control Room.*]

BURDICK: He mustn't! We need time!

TRELEAVEN: It's his decision. By all the rules he's in command of the airplane. [*Into mike.*] 714, your message is understood. Good luck to us all. Listening out. [*To* BURDICK *and* CONTROLLER.] Let's go!

[DISSOLVE TO: *the flight deck.*]

SPENCER: This is it, Doctor. You'd better go back now and make sure everybody's strapped in tight. Are both the pilots in seats?

BAIRD: Yes.

SPENCER: How about the passengers who aren't sick? Are they worried?

BAIRD: A little, but there's no panic. I exaggerated your qualifications. I'd better go. Good luck.

SPENCER [*with ironic grin*]**:** Thanks.

[DISSOLVE TO: *the Control Tower, Vancouver Airport. It is*

87

a glass-enclosed area, with radio panels and other equipment, and access is by a stairway from below. It is now daylight and the TOWER CONTROLLER *is looking skywards, using binoculars. There is the sound of hurried feet on the stairway and* TRELEAVEN, *the* CONTROLLER *and* BURDICK *emerge in that order.*]

TOWER CONTROLLER: There he is!

[TRELEAVEN *picks up a second pair of binoculars, looks through them quickly, then puts them down.*]

TRELEAVEN: All right—let's make our decision on the runway. What's it to be?

TOWER CONTROLLER: Zero eight. It's pretty well into wind now, though there'll be a slight crosswind from the right. It's also the longest.

TRELEAVEN [*into mike*]: Hullo, Flight 714. This is Martin Treleaven in Vancouver Tower. Do you read me? Over.

[CUT TO: *the flight deck.*]

STEWARDESS [*into mike*]: Yes, Vancouver Tower. Loud and clear. Over.

[CUT TO: *the Tower.*]

TRELEAVEN [*crisply, authoritatively, yet calmly*]: From here on, do not acknowledge any further transmissions unless you wish to ask a question. You are now ready to join the airport circuit. The runway for landing is zero eight. That means you are now crosswind and will shortly make a left turn on to the downwind leg. Begin now to lose height to 1,000 feet. Throttle back slightly and make your descent at 400 feet a minute. Let your air speed come back to 160 knots and hold it steady there . . . Air speed 160.

CONTROLLER [*reaching for phone*]: Runway is zero eight. All vehicles stand by near the extreme south end. Do not, repeat not, go down the runway until the aircraft has passed by you because it may swing off. Is that clear? [*Pause.*] Right.

[CUT TO: *film insert—fire trucks and ambulances are manned and move away with sirens wailing.*

[CUT TO: *the flight deck.* SPENCER *is pushing the throttles forward and the tempo of the motors increases.*]

SPENCER: Tell them we're at 1,000 feet and levelling off.

STEWARDESS [*into mike*]: Vancouver Tower. We are now at one thousand feet and levelling off. Over.

TRELEAVEN'S VOICE: Now let's have 20 degrees of flap. Do not acknowledge this message.

SPENCER: 20 degrees of flap, Janet.

[*The* STEWARDESS *reaches for flap lever and pushes it down while she watches the flap indicator.*]

TRELEAVEN'S VOICE: When you have your flaps down, bring your air speed back slowly to 140 knots, adjust your trim, and begin to make a left turn on to the downwind leg. When you have turned, fly parallel with the runway you see on your left. I repeat—air speed 140 and begin a left turn.

[CUT TO: *close-up of instrument panel showing artificial horizon and air-speed indicator. The air speed first comes back to 140, goes slightly below it, then returns to 140. The artificial horizon tilts so that the airplane symbol is banked to the left.*

[CUT TO: *the flight deck.* SPENCER *has control yoke turned to the left and is adjusting the throttles.*

[CUT TO: *the Tower.*]

TRELEAVEN: Watch your height! Don't make that turn so steep! Watch your height! More throttle! Keep the air speed on 140 and the nose up! Get back that height! You need a thousand feet!

[CUT TO: *the flight deck.* SPENCER *eases the throttles open and the tempo of the motors increases. He eases the control column forward, then pulls back again.*

[CUT TO: *close-up of a climb and descent indicator. The instrument first shows a descent of 500-feet-per-minute drop, then a climb of 600 feet, and then gradually begins to level off.*

[CUT TO: *the Control Tower.* CAPTAIN TRELEAVEN *is looking out through binoculars, the others anxiously behind him.*]

TRELEAVEN [*angrily*]: He can't fly the bloody thing! Of course

89

he can't fly it! You're watching 50 people going to their deaths!

BURDICK [*shouting*]: Keep talking to him! Keep talking! Tell him what to do!

TRELEAVEN [*urgently, into mike*]: Spencer, you can't come straight in! You've got to do some circuits, and practice that approach. You've enough fuel left for three hours' flying. Stay up, man! Stay up!

[CUT TO: *the flight deck.*]

SPENCER: Give it to me! [*Taking the mike. Then tensely.*] Listen, down there! I'm coming in! Do you hear me?—I'm coming in. There are people up here who'll die in less than an hour, never mind three. I may bend your precious airplane a bit, but I'll get it down. Now get on with the landing check. I'm putting the gear down now. [*To* STEWARDESS.] Wheels down, Janet!

[*The* STEWARDESS *selects landing gear "down" and* SPENCER *reaches for the throttles.*

[CUT TO: *airplane in flight, daylight. Its landing wheels come down.*

[CUT TO: *the flight deck.*]

STEWARDESS [*looks out of window, then back to* SPENCER]: Wheels down and three green lights.

[CUT TO: *the Tower.*]

BURDICK: He may not be able to fly worth a damn, but he's sure got guts.

TRELEAVEN [*into mike*]: Increase your throttle setting slightly to hold your air speed now that the wheels are down. Adjust your trim and keep that height at a thousand feet. Now check your propeller setting and your mixture—propellers to fully fine; mixture to full rich. I'll repeat that. Propellers to fully fine; mixture to full rich.

[CUT TO: *the flight deck.*]

SPENCER [*to himself, as he moves controls*]: Propellers fully fine. Mixture full rich. [*To* STEWARDESS.] Janet, let me hear the air speed.

STEWARDESS: 130 . . . 125 . . . 120 . . . 125 . . . 130 . . .

[CUT TO: *the Tower.*]

TRELEAVEN [*into mike*]: You are well downwind now. You can begin to make a left turn on the crosswind leg. As you turn, begin losing height to 800 feet and let your air speed come back to 120. I'll repeat that. Start a left turn. Lose height to 800. Air speed 120. [*He picks up binoculars, then puts them down hurriedly and takes mike again.*] You are losing height too fast! You are losing height too fast! Open up! Open! Hold your height now! Keep your air speed at 120.

[CUT TO: *the flight deck.*]

STEWARDESS: 110 . . . 110 . . . 105 . . . 110 . . . 110 . . . 120 . . . 120 . . . Steady at 120.

SPENCER: What a miserable insensitive wagon this is! It doesn't respond! It doesn't respond at all!

STEWARDESS: 125 . . . 130 . . . 130 . . . Steady on 130.

[CUT TO: *the Tower.*]

TRELEAVEN: Start your turn into the wind now to line up with the runway. Make it a gentle turn—you've plenty of time. As you turn, begin losing height, about 400 feet a minute. But be ready to correct if you lose height too fast. Adjust your trim as you go. That's right! Keep turning! As soon as you've completed the turn, put down full flap and bring your air speed to 115. I'll repeat that. Let down 400 feet a minute. Full flap. Then air speed 115. [*To the others.*] Is everything ready on the field?

CONTROLLER: As ready as we'll ever be.

TRELEAVEN: Then this is it. In 60 seconds we'll know.

[CUT TO: *the flight deck.*]

SPENCER [*muttering*]: Not quite yet . . . a little more . . . that should do it. [*As he straightens out of the turn.*] Janet, give me full flap! [*The* STEWARDESS *reaches for the flap control, pushes it down, and leaves it down.*] Height and air speed!

STEWARDESS: 700 feet, speed 130 . . . 600 feet, speed 120 . . . 500 feet, speed 105 . . . We're going down too quickly!

SPENCER: I know! I know! [*He pushes throttle forward and the tempo of the motors increases.*] Keep watching it!

STEWARDESS: 450 feet, speed 100 . . . 400 feet, speed 100 . . . .

[CUT TO: *film insert—airplane (DC-4) with wheels and flaps down, on a landing approach.*

[CUT TO: *the Tower.*]

TRELEAVEN [*urgently into mike*]: Open up! Open up! You're losing height too fast! [*Pause.*] Watch the air speed! Your nose is too high! Open up quickly or she'll stall! Open up, man! Open up!

BURDICK: He heard you. He's recovering.

TRELEAVEN [*into mike*]: Maintain that height until you get closer in to the runway. But be ready to ease off gently . . . You can start now . . . Let down again . . . That looks about right . . . But watch the air speed. Your nose is creeping up . . . [*More steadily.*] Now listen carefully, George. There's a slight cross-wind on the runway and your drift is to the right. Straighten up just before you touch down, and be ready with more right rudder as soon as you *are* down. And remember to cut the switches if you land too fast. [*Pause.*] All right, your approach is good . . . Get ready to round out—now! [*Pause. Then urgently.*] You're coming in too fast! Lift the nose up!

[CUT TO: *the flight deck.*]

TRELEAVEN'S VOICE: Lift the nose up! Back on the throttles! Throttles right back! Hold her off! Not too much! Not too much! Be ready for that crosswind! Ease her down, *now!* Ease her down!

[CUT TO: *film insert—a landing wheel skimming over a runway and about to touch down. As it makes contact, rock picture to show instability.*

[CUT TO: *the flight deck. There is a heavy thud and* SPENCER *and the* STEWARDESS *are jolted in their seats. There is another, another, and another. Everything shakes.*]

SPENCER [*shouting*]: Cut the switches! Cut the switches!

[*The* STEWARDESS *reaches upward and pulls down the cage of the master switches. Instantly the heavy roar of motors stops, but there is still a whistling because the airplane is travelling fast.* SPENCER *stretches out his legs as he puts his full strength into applying the airplane toe brakes, at the same time pulling back on the control column. There is a screaming of rubber on pavement, and* SPENCER *and the* STEWARDESS *are thrown violently to the left. Then, except for the hum of the radio and gyros, there is silence as the airplane stops.*]

SPENCER [*disgustedly*]: I groundlooped! I did a lousy stinking groundloop! We're turned right around the way we came!

STEWARDESS: But we're all right! We're all right! You did it! You did it!

[*She leans over and kisses him.* SPENCER *pulls off his radio headset. Outside there is a rising note of approaching sirens. Then, from the headset we hear* CAPTAIN TRELEAVEN*'s voice.*]

TRELEAVEN'S VOICE [*exuberantly*]: Hullo, George Spencer. That was probably the lousiest landing in the history of this airport. So don't ever ask us for a job as a pilot. But there are some people here who'd like to shake you by the hand, and later on we'll buy you a drink. Stay right where you are, George! We're coming over.

[FADE OUT.]

You've Gotta Be Kidding

by Dave Barry

Humorous writer Dave Barry remembers the trouble he got into when he was young—and presents his own view of how the generations get along together.

TODAY'S SCARY TOPIC FOR PARENTS IS: What Your Children Do When You're Not Home.

I have here a letter from Buffalo, New York, from working mom Judy Price, concerning her 14-year-old son, David, "who should certainly know better, because the school keeps telling me he is a genius, but I have not seen signs of this in our normal, everyday life."

Judy states that one day when she came home from work, David met her outside and said: "Hi, Mom. Are you going in?"

(This is a bad sign, parents.)

Judy says she considered replying, "No, I thought I'd just stay here in the car all night and pull away for work in the morning."

That actually would have been a wise idea. Instead, she went inside, where she found a large black circle burned into the middle of her kitchen counter.

"DAVID," she screamed. "WHAT WERE YOU COOKING?"

The soft, timid reply came back: "A baseball."

"A *baseball*," Judy writes. "Of *course*. What else could it be? How could I forget to tell my children never to cook a baseball? It's my fault, really."

It turns out that according to David's best friend's cousin—and if you can't believe HIM, who CAN you believe?—you can hit a baseball three times as far if you really heat it up first. So David did this, and naturally he put the red-hot pan down directly onto the countertop, probably because there was no rare antique furniture available.

For the record: David claims that the heated baseball did, in fact, go farther. But this does NOT mean that you young readers should try this foolish and dangerous experiment at home. Use a friend's home.

No, seriously, you young people should never heat a baseball without proper adult supervision, just as you should never—and I say this from personal experience—attempt to make a rumba box.

A rumba box is an obscure musical instrument that consists of a wooden box with metal strips attached to it in such a way that when you plunk them, the box resonates with a pleasant rhythmic sound. The only time I ever saw a rumba box was in 1964, when a friend of my parents named Walter Karl played one at a gathering at our house, and it sounded great. Mr. Karl explained that the metal strips were actually pieces of the spring from an old-fashioned wind-up phonograph. This gave my best friend, Lanny Watts, an idea.

Lanny was always having ideas. For example, one day he got tired of walking to the end of his driveway to get the mail, so he had the idea of hanging the mailbox from a rope-and-pulley system strung up the driveway to his porch, where he hooked it up to a washing-machine motor. When the mailman came, Lanny simply plugged in the motor, and *whoosh,* the mailbox fell down. The amount of time Lanny spent unsuccessfully trying to get this labor-saving device to work was equivalent to approximately 5,000 trips to get the actual mail, but that is the price of convenience.

So anyway, when Lanny heard Mr. Karl explain the rumba box, he realized two things:

1. His parents had an old-fashioned wind-up phonograph they hardly ever used.
2. They both worked out of the home.

So Lanny and I decided to make our own rumba box. Our plan, as I recall it, was to take the phonograph apart, snip off a bit of the spring, then put the phonograph back together, and nobody would be the wiser. This plan worked perfectly until we removed the metal box that held the phonograph spring; this box turned out to be very hard to open.

"Why would they make it so *strong*?" we asked ourselves.

Finally, recalling the lessons we had learned about mechanical advantage in high-school physics class, we decided to hit the box with a sledge hammer.

Do you remember the climactic scene in the movie *Raiders of the Lost Ark,* when the Nazis open up the Ark of the Covenant and out surges a terrifying horde of evil fury and the Nazis' heads melt like chocolate bunnies in a microwave? Well, that's similar to what happened when Lanny sledge-hammered the spring box. It turns out that the reason the box is so strong is that there is a really powerful, tightly wound, extremely irritable spring in there, and when you let it out, it just goes *berserk,* writhing and snarling and thrashing violently all over the room, seeking to gain revenge on all the people who have cranked it over the years.

Lanny and I fled the room until the spring calmed down. When we returned, we found phonograph parts spread all over the room, mixed in with approximately 2.4 miles of spring. We realized we'd have to modify our Project Goal slightly, from making a rumba box to being in an entirely new continent when Lanny's mom got home.

Actually, Mrs. Watts went fairly easy on us, just as Judy Price seems to have been good-natured about her son's heating the baseball. Moms are usually pretty good that way.

But sometimes I wonder. You know how guys are always complaining that they used to have a baseball-card collection that would be worth a fortune today if they still had it, but their moms threw it out? And the guys always say, "Mom just didn't know any better."

Well, I wonder if the moms knew *exactly* what they were doing.

Getting even.

Beware: Do Not Read This Poem

by Ishmael Reed

tonite, thriller was
abt an ol woman, so vain she
surrounded herself w/
    many mirrors

it got so bad that finally she
locked herself indoors & her
whole life became the
    mirrors

one day the villagers broke
into her house , but she was too
swift for them . she disappeared
    into a mirror
each tenant who bought the house
after that , lost a loved one to

    the ol woman in the mirror :
    first a little girl
    then a young woman
    then the young woman/s husband

the hunger of this poem is legendary
it has taken in many victims
back off from this poem
it has drawn in yr feet
back off from this poem
it has drawn in yr legs

98

back off from this poem
it is a greedy mirror
you are into this poem . from
    the waist down
nobody can hear you can they ?
this poem has had you up to here
    belch
this poem aint got no manners
you cant call out frm this poem
relax now & go w/ this poem

move & roll on to this poem
do not resist this poem
this poem has yr eyes
this poem has his head
this poem has his arms
this poem has his fingers
this poem has his fingertips

this poem is the reader & the
reader this poem

statistics : the us bureau of missing persons re-
        ports that in 1968 over 100,000 people
        disappeared leaving no solid clues
           nor trace   only
   a space   in the lives of their friends

Lament

by Edna St. Vincent Millay

Listen, children:
Your father is dead.
From his old coats
I'll make you little jackets;
I'll make you little trousers
From his old pants.
There'll be in his pockets
Things he used to put there,
Keys and pennies
Covered with tobacco;
Dan shall have the pennies
To save in his bank;
Anne shall have the keys
To make a pretty noise with.
Life must go on,
And the dead be forgotten;
Life must go on,
Though good men die;
Anne, eat your breakfast;
Dan, take your medicine;
Life must go on;
I forget just why.

Thurgood Marshall: The Fight for Justice

by Rae Bains

Segregation was a system of laws that kept some Americans from participating equally in society. Thurgood Marshall spent his adult life battling that system. When he died in 1993, he left a legacy of great change for all Americans.

"Thurgood, since you won't sit still and let your class-mates do their work, take yourself to the principal's office!"

The other boys and girls giggled. Nine-year-old Thurgood Marshall pretended he didn't care as he walked slowly from the room. But he did care. He knew the punishment that was coming. He would have to stay after school and learn another part of the Constitution of the United States. That was what the principal made him do every time he acted up in class.

Another after-school ball game missed, Thurgood thought gloomily. Another hour in that hall outside the principal's office. Another page of long, hard words to learn by heart. Worst of all, another long, hard lecture at home. There was no way to hide his punishment from his parents. Mama was a teacher in the Division Street school, and she'd *know!*

Thurgood got into trouble so often, he had memorized all of the Constitution except for some of the amendments at the end. And little by little, he was working his way through those. This afternoon his assignment was the Fourteenth Amendment.

The boy read the first part of the amendment. He read it again, out loud. He thought about the words he was saying. They seemed very important.

That night, at dinner, Thurgood sat quietly through his parents' lecture. Finally, he said, "I'm sorry." Then he asked about something that had been on his mind since that afternoon. "What does the Fourteenth Amendment mean when it says that a state can't deny anybody 'the equal protection of the laws'? Doesn't that mean the laws should be equal for Negroes and white people? So why can't I sit anywhere I want to at the ball park? Or on the trolley car?"

William Marshall was proud that Thurgood thought about important things. But he was sad that such questions had to be asked. "The Constitution is good," he said. "The words say how things *should* be. Maybe there is no equality for Negroes today. But someday, because of the Constitution, there will be equality."

"The Constitution is a guide," Norma Marshall said. "It's like a rule book for Americans. The country doesn't always follow the rules, but they are there. And as your father said, someday...."

Thurgood enjoyed the talks at the dinner table. His parents were smart and fair. And they worked so hard—Mama at teaching, Papa as chief steward of a big country club. The Marshalls were respected members of their Baltimore, Maryland, community.

Norma and William Marshall had high hopes for their sons. They decided that William Aubrey, born in 1904, was going to be a doctor. Thoroughgood, born on July 2, 1908, and named after his Grandpa Marshall, was going to be a dentist. In those days, many white doctors and dentists did not treat black people. There was a real need in the black community for well-trained professionals. The Marshalls wanted their sons to help meet that need.

The Marshall family lived in a pleasant, middle-class neighborhood in West Baltimore. Black children and white children played together on the street in front of their houses. But they went to separate schools.

While he was growing up, young Thurgood (he shortened his name when he was in second grade) saw segregation every day of his life. But it didn't make him feel like a second-class citizen. That was because his parents taught him he was as good as anyone. If he was honest and fair and worked hard, he was anyone's equal—no matter what the law said.

As a teenager, Thurgood still planned to become a dentist. But, thanks to his father, he became more interested in the legal system. Mr. Marshall liked to go to the courthouse and listen to the cases being tried. Whenever possible, Thurgood went with him. They often discussed the trials and verdicts at dinner time. "My father never told me to become a lawyer," Thurgood Marshall said later, "but he turned me into one. He did it by teaching me to argue, by challenging my logic on every point, by making me prove every statement I made."

Thurgood Marshall was proud of his father. One reason was that William Marshall was the first black person to serve on a Baltimore grand jury. A grand jury listens to all the facts when someone is charged with a crime. Then it decides if there is enough evidence to put the accused person on trial.

The first time Mr. Marshall was a grand juror, something bothered him. He noticed that his fellow jurors always asked if the accused person was black or white. He also noticed that black people were more often sent to trial than white people. If the accused person was white, the case was often dismissed.

Mr. Marshall objected to this. He said it was wrong to ask a person's color before deciding if there was a case against that person. The other grand jurors said nothing. They were shocked that a black man had the nerve to object to the system.

Then the foreman of the grand jury made a ruling. The question of race was not to be asked again.

This example of his father's courage filled young Thurgood with admiration. It also showed how important it was for black people to become involved in the legal system. It was clear that blacks had to speak up for their rights if they wanted justice and equality.

When Thurgood graduated from high school in 1925, he followed his brother, Aubrey, to Lincoln University. Lincoln was a small school in Pennsylvania. It had about 300 students, all black men, and an all-white teaching staff. The standards were high and the courses were difficult. Aubrey Marshall did very well at Lincoln. After graduation, he went to medical school and became a highly respected surgeon.

At Lincoln, Thurgood did enough studying to earn a B average. But he didn't spend all his time with books. There were sports, the debating team, pep rallies, parties, dances, and fraternity activities.

In Thurgood Marshall's second year at Lincoln, he got into trouble for taking part in a fraternity prank. The school suspended him and his friends. Marshall did a lot of thinking. He thought about his parents saving their money for his college costs. He thought about the summer months and after-school hours he had worked to pay some of his school bills. He had worked as a grocery clerk, baker, waiter, delivery boy, and bellhop. Getting thrown out of school for fooling around was childish, he realized. Marshall decided it was time to grow up.

When he returned to Lincoln, the "new" Marshall threw himself into serious studying. He read the works of black novelists, poets, and scholars. Their ideas led him to take a closer look at the life of blacks in America. Marshall and his college friends wanted to be successful, to earn a good income, and to win respect in society. But they also saw their responsibility. They had to do something for blacks who did not have the same chance to go to college as they had.

Racial discrimination weighed heavily on every black

American. In the South, the laws kept blacks from enjoying equal rights. And even though there were no segregation laws in the North, blacks did not enjoy equal treatment there.

Right near Lincoln University there was a segregated movie theater. Local custom said that blacks weren't allowed to sit downstairs. They had to sit in the balcony. One night Thurgood Marshall and a group of his friends decided to challenge this custom. They went to the theater and sat in the "whites only" orchestra seats.

An usher told the young men to go upstairs. Marshall said, "I paid for my ticket and I'm going to stay where I am." Marshall and his friends watched the movie with everyone else. "The amazing thing was," he wrote to his parents, "when we were leaving we just walked out with those other people and they didn't do anything, didn't say a thing, didn't even look at us—at least, as far as I know. I'm not sure I like being invisible, but maybe it's better than being put to shame and not able to respect yourself."

At the beginning of Marshall's third year of college, he met Vivian Burey, a senior at the University of Pennsylvania. Vivian was called "Buster" by her friends. Thurgood and Buster met at Cherry Street Memorial Church, fell in love soon after, and were married in September, 1929. Their marriage lasted until Mrs. Marshall died 26 years later.

Thurgood Marshall graduated with honors in June, 1930. During his senior year at Lincoln, he had decided not to be a dentist. He wanted to be a lawyer. It was something he had been building toward all his life: learning the Constitution in grammar school; the dinner-time discussions with his parents; the trials he attended with his father; the debating team in college; integrating the local movie theater; reading about the black struggle in America. Marshall was sure that the law was the key to equality for his people.

Marshall applied to the University of Maryland's law school. But because he was black, his application was turned down. So he enrolled in Howard University's law school in Washington,

D.C. Howard was founded in 1867 to educate former slaves. Since that time, thousands of black doctors, dentists, lawyers, and other professionals have graduated from Howard.

Thurgood and Buster Marshall lived with his parents in Baltimore while he attended law school. Everyone in the family helped pay his school expenses. Norma Marshall sold some of her jewelry. Buster Marshall took a job as a secretary. William Marshall contributed a share of his salary. Thurgood Marshall got up at 5:30 every morning and took a train to Washington. He attended classes until 3:00 in the afternoon, took the train back to Baltimore, and went to work at one of several part-time jobs. At night, he studied until after midnight.

The work and school schedule was so hard that the 6'2" tall student went from 170 pounds to 130. But he finished his freshman year first in his class. In Marshall's second year at Howard, he was given the job of assistant in the law library. The job paid his school costs for the next two years, but it kept him in Washington until late at night. During this time, the hard-working young man got to know Charles Houston. Houston was a dean at Howard's law school and a leading civil rights activist.

When Marshall graduated from law school in 1933, he opened a law office in Baltimore. But he had two strikes against him. It was the middle of the Great Depression, and few people had money to hire a lawyer. White people never hired black lawyers in those days. Even black people preferred white lawyers. At the end of his first year, Marshall showed a total loss of $1,000.

In 1934, guided by Charles Houston, Marshall became the official lawyer for the Baltimore branch of the National Association for the Advancement of Colored People (NAACP). This was the real beginning of his legal career. The next year, Marshall and Houston took on a major civil rights case.

Donald G. Murray was a black Maryland college graduate. Murray had applied to the University of Maryland's law school. Like Marshall, he was turned down because he was black.

Marshall and Houston took the University of Maryland to court. They did not fight the segregation laws directly. Instead, they focused on the "separate but equal" decisions of the U. S. Supreme Court. "Separate but equal" meant that states were allowed to set up separate schools for both races, so long as the schools were equal. Of course, everyone knew that blacks and whites did not get equal educations. But that was hard to prove in court.

There was only one law school in Maryland, so there was no doubt that Murray was denied an equal opportunity for education. The court gave the State of Maryland two choices: admit Donald Murray to the law school, or provide a law school for black Maryland college graduates. Since it was too expensive to open a second law school, the school had to admit Murray to the University of Maryland. It was Thurgood Marshall's first great legal victory. In the courtroom, he showed no emotion when the verdict was read. But as soon as he got outside, he threw his arms around his wife and began to dance.

The Murray case was just the beginning for Marshall. Over the next few years, he chipped away at school segregation. In case after case, in Missouri, in Texas, and all over the South, Marshall and the NAACP challenged segregation laws. Each time, they did it by showing that qualified black students did not have equal opportunity for higher education. Each time, the cases were lost in the lower courts. And each time, the U.S. Supreme Court reversed the decision, giving the final victory to Marshall.

In 1938, Marshall became the NAACP's chief counsel. His headquarters were in New York. But he didn't spend much time there. He traveled around the country, going wherever black Americans needed a strong legal voice.

Marshall was always prepared when he went into court, and his courtroom efforts were brilliant. In his years as NAACP counsel, he won 29 cases before the Supreme Court!

State after state felt the effects of Marshall's legal crusade. Segregation laws took a beating at his hands. But the laws remained on the books. Black people were still segregated. That had to end, Marshall vowed. "The terms 'separate' and 'equal' cannot be used together," he said. "There can be no separate equality."

Marshall and the NAACP Legal Defense Fund decided to challenge school segregation at all levels. They did this in a case that is known as *Brown v. Board of Education.* (The letter *v.* stands for *versus,* the Latin word for "against.") There were actually five cases presented to the Supreme Court in 1952 as part of *Brown.* These cases came from Delaware, Virginia, Kansas, Washington, D.C., and South Carolina.

In each case, Marshall and his fellow lawyers attacked the very idea of school segregation. It took a year and a half before the Supreme Court handed down its decision. In May, 1954, the highest court in the land declared that school segregation was against the law. "Separate but equal" was not acceptable anymore. Thurgood Marshall was "so happy, I was numb."

But it was only half a victory. A year later, the Supreme Court ruled that the states had to make plans to integrate their schools but did not have to do this right away. The battle was far from over.

Marshall fought segregation on many fronts. There were cases seeking equal rights for blacks in public housing, public parks, sports arenas, and public transportation. Marshall and his fellow lawyers went after every law that discriminated against black people or any other minority.

In 1961, Thurgood Marshall was appointed a judge on the U.S. Court of Appeals. This court is one level below the U.S. Supreme Court. Marshall served as an appeals judge for four years. In 1965, President Lyndon Johnson offered Marshall the job of Solicitor General of the United States. The Solicitor General represents the United States in cases that appear before the Supreme Court. Marshall was proud to accept the position. As Solicitor General, he made sure that the Civil Rights Act of 1964 was obeyed. This was what both President Johnson and Marshall wanted—equal rights for *all* Americans.

In 1967, President Johnson appointed Thurgood Marshall to the Supreme Court of the United States. Johnson said, "I believe it is the right thing to do, the right time to do it, the right man and the right place. I believe he has already earned his place in history, but I think it will be greatly enhanced by his service on the Court."

Thurgood Marshall became the 96th justice to take the oath, and the first black justice in the 178 years of the Supreme Court's history. It was the start of a distinguished career that lasted until Marshall retired in 1991.

During his years on the Court, Marshall remained a powerful spokesman for equal rights, for the freedoms guaranteed by the Constitution, and for peaceful change. As he said, "It takes no courage to get in the back of a crowd and throw a rock. Rather, it takes courage to stand up on your two feet and look anyone straight in the eye and say, 'I will not be beaten.' I say to you . . . move, but move within the Constitution, and find new ways of moving nonviolently within the Constitution, bearing in mind that there are many of us in this country who will not let it go down the drain."

After Marshall's retirement, Justice Sandra Day O'Connor, another member of the Supreme Court, spoke about his great influence on the Court and its decisions. "Justice Marshall," she said, "imparted not only his legal knowledge but also his life experiences, pushing and prodding us to respond . . . to the power of moral truth."

Thurgood Marshall once said, "The true miracle of the Constitution was not its birth but its life." He spent his life defending that belief.

Everything Became a Secret: Paulette Pomeranz' Story

by Maxine Rosenberg

What would you do if someone you cared for was being hunted? What if you knew that person was innocent? During World War II, some people risked their lives to hide children from the Nazis. Paulette Pomeranz was one of those children. She told the true story of her experiences to writer Maxine Rosenberg.

When I was very young, my parents got divorced. My mother ran her own business, and she found it too hard to take care of me. Instead, I went to live with Eli, one of her workers, and Eli's family. Their religion was Greek Orthodox, and they had a house ten minutes from Athens, the city where I was born and where my mother had her store.

For the next three years, while Eli's mother, Julia, watched me, my mother visited a lot, and my father and older brother, Daniel, who lived with him, came to see me too.

Then in 1941, when I was seven and a half, Greece was divided up between Germany and Italy. The Italians, who were in charge of Athens, pretty much left the Jews alone. But things were very dangerous in the German-occupied areas. In Salonika, where my relatives and most Greek Jews lived, Jews were being rounded up and taken away.

One night my mother came by and woke me. She said she was leaving to find a safer country for us and that she would soon return for me. I was so sleepy, I didn't know what she was talking about.

A few months later I heard shouting in the house. "The Germans are here! They're all over the place," Julia was screaming in panic. She had no idea where my mother was and didn't know what to do with me.

By then we had become very attached. After living with her for so long, I called her "Mama." On Sundays I went to church with her and her daughters. But I was still Jewish, and Julia was worried. The next morning she took me to a synagogue so we could talk to a rabbi.

It was the first time I had ever been inside a synagogue. Since my family didn't observe our religion or celebrate any of the holidays, I knew more about Greek Orthodoxy than I did about Judaism.

Julia told the rabbi that she had heard rumors about Germans rounding up Jews and asked whether she should have me baptized for safety. The rabbi said, "Do what you must to protect the child."

As soon as we got home, Julia gave me a cross and told me I had to wear it all the time. She also said that when I left the house I was always to stay with my friend Athena, who was five years older than I. Athena knew I was Jewish and was going to watch out for me.

Meanwhile Julia warned me not to give out any information about our lives. No one was to know we had visited the rabbi or what went on inside our house. Everything became a secret.

In 1943 the Italian government fell, and the Germans took over the rest of Greece. They set up headquarters in my school, across the street from our house. Every time I walked by, I was terrified. I was sure a German would grab me and take me away on a train.

The townspeople were frightened too. Although I was the

only Jewish person in the neighborhood, they knew that if the Germans found out, we'd all be shot. Yet they did everything to help me. One day the baker told Julia that if I were ever in serious danger, I should go directly to his shop, and he'd show me an escape route he had mapped out.

Still, I could never relax. At night I kept my shoes and winter coat next to my bed in case of an emergency.

By then there were tremendous food shortages. Sometimes we had so little to eat, Julia would count out raisins for dinner. She'd hand me most of her portion and say, "I'm not hungry."

Usually, though, there was some rice, soup, vegetables, or bread. But other people in town weren't as lucky. I was afraid one of them might denounce me for a cup of flour or a tablespoon of sugar.

Meanwhile I got a letter from my mother telling me she was in America. She said that when the war was over, she'd send for me. Now I had no idea when I'd see her, or my father and Daniel, who were running from place to place trying to hide from the Germans.

At least I had Julia. She treated me like a princess. Whenever she'd get a piece of material, she'd sew me pretty clothes and tie ribbons in my hair. She also did everything to keep me safe. But I wasn't sure what she'd do if the situation got too dangerous.

I tried to please her to make sure she'd never send me away. I volunteered to wash the floors, make the beds, and run errands. When the Germans started taking all the bread from the bakery, I got up before dawn, slipped into the shop, and left with a small loaf the baker had given me hidden under my arm. I wanted Julia to see I was a good girl and that she needed me.

Now that the Germans occupied my school, I only went to makeshift classes twice a week in the church basement. The other days I played ball or hide-and-seek with my friends. Mostly we talked about food when we were together. When my friends asked what I wished I could eat at that very moment, I always said white bread, sugar, and chocolate.

Sometimes a neighbor would hear what was being sold on the black market and would tell Athena and me. We'd go to that person's house or meet on the corner to make a deal. I'd ask, "How much do you want for a glass of oil?" and the person would say, "How about a carton of cigarettes?" More often I had money or a tiny piece of gold that Julia had given me, and I'd trade with that. I was good at this job, and that pleased Julia.

One night there was loud knocking on the door. When Julia looked out the window, she saw two Gestapo officers, each with a barking German shepherd on a leash. "Get under the covers and pretend you're asleep," she told me.

The German officers said they had found a parachute and were looking for the British paratrooper who owned it. Julia said she knew nothing about this and offered them coffee. As they sat around the table, they showed her pictures of their families.

In 1944 the Allies started bombing Athens. Whenever the sirens sounded, everybody ran for shelter to an open trench in the town square. Our only protection was cooking pots we wore on our heads. My helmet was a frying pan that I kept under my bed. I tried to make a game of the whole thing, but I was scared. I never knew if I'd reach the trench in time.

All the while Julia kept trying to give me hope. She'd describe how wonderful America was and tell me that one day I'd live there and have everything I could want. Although I didn't want to leave Julia, the fantasy of becoming an actress and being rich appealed to me. I'd have enough money to send Julia a nice warm coat for the winter.

Meanwhile my life was very difficult. My shoes had worn out, and the soles flopped when I walked. My coat too was threadbare, so Julia put newspapers inside my clothing to keep me warm. "Just wait till you get to America," she kept saying. But sometimes I wasn't sure I would last long enough to make it there.

Then one day I overheard Julia tell her daughters that all of my relatives in Salonika had perished. By this same time my father and Daniel had stopped visiting. I was frightened that something bad must have happened to them too.

To make things worse, the bombing increased and lots of British planes were being shot down. In the morning my friends and I would see white parachutes lying in the street and race out to grab them before they were found by the Germans. As Julia cut and sewed the parachutes to make sheets and dresses for me, the two of us would try to figure out who was hiding the men. If we saw someone buying extra food, we'd suspect that family. Naturally we kept this a secret too.

Suddenly, one summer morning in 1945, I woke up and noticed that the Germans had vacated my school. They must have left in the night. Whatever, it was the last I ever saw of them. The next thing I knew, English tanks were on the road, and the soldiers were throwing chocolates and caramels to everyone. It was the first time since the war had begun that people acted happy.

A few months later I got a letter from my mother, saying she was trying to get papers for me to come to America. After that she sent a package through the Red Cross. It contained a skirt, a jacket, shoes, a sweater, and a volleyball. Now I was the queen of the neighborhood.

Six to eight months later my mother wrote again, this time to say she was coming to Greece to take me back with her to America. Also, my father and Daniel visited me. Daniel, who was 19, was leaving for Palestine, where many Jewish children were settling. He and my father wanted to know if I'd like to go too, but Julia said no.

Then one day my mother arrived, and Julia and I went to the boat to meet her. I recognized her from the photos Julia had shown me over the years, but when she kissed me hello, I felt I was greeting a stranger.

It took some months before my mother could get me a ticket to America. Finally, in January 1947, everything was ready. I was then 13 years old.

"I'll send you clothes and food from America," I told Julia and my friends as they hugged me good-bye. They were all crying, but I felt nothing. I was like a robot.

For the next year in America, I refused to unpack my suitcase. I was determined to go back to Greece and wrote to Julia and my friends telling them how lonely I was. At Eastertime Julia sent me a tin of my favorite cookies, which made me miss her even more.

In the meantime my mother remarried, and within a few years she had two more children. We kids became close, but I still kept thinking about Julia and my friends in Greece. Finally, in 1958, my mother said Julia could come visit us, and she helped pay the fare.

Julia liked America so much, she decided to stay, and soon her daughters joined her. After that I had my two mothers in America and my Greek family nearby.

POSTSCRIPT

Until she died a few months ago at age 93, Julia and I lived near each other. I visited her a couple of times a week, and I continued to call her "Mama." My children called her "Yaya," which is Greek for *grandmother.*

My family celebrated the Greek holidays with her, and when I started observing Jewish holidays, she and her family were at our Passover table.

I was with Julia to the end of her life. She was my other mother. She gave me a home and affection and kept me safe. I could never repay her for what she had done.

Ordeal in the Owyhee Country

by Margaret Truman Daniel

*In this true story of a Paiute heroine, a brave woman
risks capture by enemies of her people. Can Sarah
Winnemucca sneak through enemy lines to save her
father and her people from a war they want to avoid?*

As anyone who has ever seen a cowboy movie knows, two basic ingredients of courage in a crisis are daring and physical prowess. How often have we watched western heroes from William S. Hart to John Wayne display their nerve and muscles in exclusively male duels to the death. In the mythical old West, men were men and women were hardly visible. But in the real West, a woman once displayed more daring and endurance than all the males in sight.

Sarah Winnemucca's Indian name was Thocmetony or Shell Flower. She belonged to a tribe called the Southern Paiutes who lived in what is now the state of Nevada. I don't know which tribe suffered more injustices at the hands of the white men but I would venture to guess that the Southern Paiutes must be near the top of the list. The most tragic part of their agony is that they were docile, peace-loving people who wanted nothing more than to work their farms and live in harmony with their neighbors.

The Southern Paiutes had their first contact with white men in the early 1840s when small groups of traders and explorers began trickling into Nevada and setting up outposts on Paiute lands. Sarah, who was only a child at the time, was petrified of the newcomers with their noisy guns and pale skins, but the rest of the Southern Paiutes welcomed the white settlers.

The friendship was cemented when, in the winter of 1845, Sarah's grandfather, Chief Winnemucca, accompanied Captain John Fremont on an expedition across the Sierra Nevada Mountains to California. Winnemucca returned full of admiration for the white man's ways. Unfortunately, by the time he died in 1860, the spirit of trust and goodwill that had existed between the two peoples was beginning to disintegrate.

Another tribe of Nevada Indians, who were more warlike than the Southern Paiutes, had become involved in several skirmishes with the white settlers. After one particularly bloody encounter, the whites herded all the Indians in the region onto the Pyramid Lake Reservation in northern Nevada.

The Southern Paiutes were told that the move would be to their advantage. They would be given larger and more productive farms, and the government would supply them with food and clothing. As it turned out, the Indian agent who ran the reservation had little interest in his charges' welfare. He cheated them out of their rations and spent most of his time scheming to line his own pockets at their expense. Sarah Winnemucca was the only member of her tribe who was not shocked at the white man's duplicity.

Sarah had lost her childhood fear of whites after she became ill with a mysterious fever and a white woman nursed her back to health. Later, as a teenager, she had lived with the family of a white stage-company agent and served as a companion to his daughter. By then, Sarah had forgotten her earlier antipathy to whites. She learned to speak English, dropped her Indian name of Thocmetony, and assumed the Christian name Sarah.

Chief Winnemucca was so pleased to see his granddaughter adopting the ways of his friends, the whites, that he decreed on his deathbed that she continue her education at St. Mary's Convent School in San Jose, California. The 16-year-old had barely arrived when the parents of white students began complaining about sending their daughters to school with an Indian girl. Three weeks later, Sarah Winnemucca was on her way back to Nevada. Her early distrust of whites had returned, but this time it was more than a childhood phobia; she had good reason to view them with a wary eye.

Sarah's father, Winnemucca II, was now chief of the Southern Paiutes. Not knowing how to deal with the unscrupulous Indian agent at Pyramid Lake, the chief and his tribe had solved the problem by wandering away from the reservation and attaching themselves to a nearby army post. Contrary to the usual image of the U.S. Cavalry as bloodthirsty Indian haters, the soldiers treated the Paiutes kindly, sharing their rations and finding odd jobs for them at the post. Sarah, who had a natural gift for languages, became an interpreter. She knew three different Indian tongues and had mastered Spanish as well as English.

In 1875, the Southern Paiutes were finally given an official home. The government moved them to a vast tract of land in southeast Oregon called Malheur Reservation. The soil was good, the climate pleasant, and although they were still under the supervision of the government, their new agent, Samuel Parrish, was that rarity in the Indian Bureau, an honest and sympathetic man. He saw to it that his charges were well supplied with food and clothing, assigned them individual grain fields, and allowed them to keep the crops they raised. Under Parrish's supervision, the Paiutes worked hard and took pride in their farms. It was a bitter blow to them when Parrish was abruptly removed and a new agent, William V. Rinehart, appointed in his place.

Like most Indian agents, Rinehart had obtained his position

through political influence and had no interest in the Indians or their problems. He abolished the individual farms, made all the Indians work for him and, instead of wages, paid them for their labor with the food and clothing that were supposed to be given to them as gifts from the government.

Several other Indian tribes also lived at Malheur. One of them, the Northern Paiutes, expressed their contempt for William Rinehart by walking off the reservation and joining forces with the Bannock Indians in neighboring Idaho, who were preparing to go on the warpath.

The Southern Paiutes took a less aggressive approach to their problems. Since Sarah Winnemucca knew the white man's tongue, they asked her to be their spokesman. She went to the nearest army camp and asked the commanding officer to appeal to the federal government on behalf of her people for the dismissal of Rinehart and the reappointment of Samuel Parrish. The government ignored the request and worse yet, informed William Rinehart that Sarah Winnemucca had organized a plot against him. The infuriated agent vowed to be even tougher with the Paiutes and began by banishing Sarah from Malheur.

A few weeks later, in June 1878, the Bannock uprising began. Sarah had gone to live with some of her tribesmen in the John Day Valley, not far from the reservation. She learned about the uprising only by accident. She had been hired to drive two white men and one of their daughters from Oregon to Silver City, Idaho. Sarah had taken the wagon trail to Silver City many times before. There were a number of settlements along the way where travelers stopped to rest and exchange news with the inhabitants. On this trip, however, the settlements were deserted. There were no men working in the fields, no women hanging out washing, no children playing in the yard.

The four travelers heard the clopping of horses' hooves in the distance. A detachment of cavalry came galloping up the road. Their commanding officer gravely informed Sarah and her passengers that they were traveling at the risk of their lives. The

Bannock Indians were on the warpath. All the white settlers in the region had taken refuge at Fort Lyon, a few miles away. The soldiers urged the travelers to do the same.

At the army post, Sarah learned more about the Bannock uprising. It had started with an attack on some white families on Big Camas Prairie a few days before. Next, the Bannocks captured a stagecoach bringing military supplies to the fort. They seized two boxes of Winchester rifles and hundreds of rounds of ammunition.

Sarah was not surprised to learn that the Northern Paiutes, who had left Malheur Reservation in rebellion against William Rinehart, had become the Bannocks' allies in their war against the whites. She was horrified at the next piece of news. A raiding party of Northern Paiutes had swooped down on Malheur, kidnapped a large band of Southern Paiutes, including Sarah's father and brother, and forced them to join the Bannock camp.

Sarah was not the only one who was upset at this news. The commanding officer at Fort Lyon, the former Civil War hero General O. O. Howard, had been trying for days to contact Chief Winnemucca II. He wanted to let him know that the army was aware that he and his people were unwilling captives and to tell him that if they could escape from the Bannocks and reach Fort Lyon, the soldiers would see that they were well treated.

General Howard tried to find someone to take his message to the Southern Paiutes. The scouts and trappers who were usually available for such missions refused. The Bannocks had taken their prisoners to a hiding place high in the mountains of present-day Owyhee County, Idaho, over a hundred miles away. Whoever made the trip would have to contend with some of the most forbidding terrain in America, a landscape of black basalt bluffs towering against pale washes, where even sagebrush and greasewood grow precariously. If a messenger reached the Bannock encampment, how would he get his message to Chief Winnemucca? The Bannocks were sure to have sharp-eyed warriors continuously studying the barren landscape. Any outsider would be killed on sight.

Aside from the problem of finding the Bannock camp, General Howard was loath to attack it while the friendly Southern Paiutes were captives. They might be the worst sufferers in a pitched battle. He asked Sarah if she would volunteer to carry his message of peace and refuge to her father.

Howard was asking a 34-year-old woman to undertake a journey that had already scared off a half dozen rugged frontiersmen. A 34-year-old Indian woman who had experienced the cruel prejudice that infected the minds of too many white Americans. It is not hard to imagine the welter of conflicting emotions that must have assailed Sarah Winnemucca. A white man was asking her to undertake a suicide mission. If she agreed, there was a very good chance that she would die of starvation wandering through the unmapped, desolate lava wastes of the Owyhee country. If she refused, she might have to live with the knowledge that her father, her brother, and several dozen members of her tribe had died because she did not try to save them.

In the beginning, a voice deep inside Sarah Winnemucca must have snarled a silent NO to General Howard's request. There were plenty of reasons to suspect the offer, beyond her already strong distrust of white men. What if the General was only using her to start a civil war between her father's people and the Bannocks? If the Indians started killing each other, it would be that much easier for the cavalry to finish them off.

But Oliver O. Howard was no ordinary general. A gentle, deeply religious man, he had been a leading supporter of bringing black Americans into the Union army during the Civil War and keeping them there after the war. For him, the great conflict had been a crusade against slavery. He had paid a price for his commitment; one sleeve of his uniform was empty. Without making speeches, Howard communicated his passionate belief in human equality, regardless of skin color, to Sarah Winnemucca. Supporting this fragile trust was the profound tribal loyalty that was part of Sarah's Indian heritage.

121

Most whites find it hard to understand this feeling of community. To Sarah Winnemucca, daughter and granddaughter of chiefs, it was as natural as breathing. Woven through her childhood were memories of tribal celebrations in which women played prominent roles. Her favorite was the Festival of Flowers, when the young girls gathered blossoms and wove them into garlands. "Come and be happy with me," they had sung. "I shall be beautiful while the earth lasts. Dance and be happy with me."

In the name of this lost happiness and her heritage as the daughter of a chief, Sarah Winnemucca accepted the responsibility the white General asked her to take. On a horse supplied by Howard, she set out for the Bannock camp with two Indian scouts, John and George Paiute, as guides. They rode along the banks of the Owyhee River for about 15 miles until they came to the remains of a Bannock campsite. There were clumps of hair on the ground, and strings of beads had been broken and scattered around—part of the Bannock mourning ritual for a slain chief.

"The Bannocks' chief, Buffalo Horn, must have been killed in the fighting," Sarah said with a shudder. There was no need to add that the trip would be even more perilous now because the Bannocks would be eager to avenge his death.

A few miles farther along, Sarah and her companions stopped to rest at a deserted farmhouse. Everything flammable, furniture, bedding, and clothes, had been hauled out of the house, piled in the yard, and burned. The fire was still smoldering when they rode up, and there were fresh footprints in the soil. The Bannocks had obviously left only a short time before.

Soon after, the travelers came to a fork in the road. One of the paths was a newly blazed trail that led straight into the mountains. They took it and, a few miles later, came across further ominous evidence that they were on the right track. On the side of the road, they found a stage driver's whip, a clock, and a fiddle. Sarah had no doubts that the owners of all three items were no longer alive to claim them.

The trail grew steeper and more treacherous. Several times, Sarah was almost pitched out of the saddle when her horse lost his footing on the bare stone. Washington Irving, on a trip West, had visited this part of Idaho and described it as "a vast uninhabited solitude, with precipitous cliffs and yawning ravines, looking like the ruins of a world." The trail wound along huge granite scarps and ledges over 1,000-foot gorges cut by creeks whose waters barely saw the sun. It was a desert, not of sand, but of rock, uninhabited by man. The sun beat down on the riders, as pitiless as the landscape through which they toiled.

Suddenly Sarah's guides reined in their horses. They pointed to two figures on the slope of a mountain in the distance. They were definitely Indians, but from the distance it was hard to tell whether they were Bannocks or Paiutes. Gambling on the hope that they were fellow tribesmen, Sarah called and waved her handkerchief. As they drew closer, she was relieved to see that not only were they Paiutes but one of them was her brother Lee.

Although Lee was happy to see Sarah, he had only bad news to give her. "Our people are all prisoners of the Bannocks," he reported mournfully. "They have been stripped of their weapons; their horses and blankets have been taken, and they have been very badly treated."

When Sarah told Lee that she had come to bring a message to their father, he could only shake his head. "The Bannocks will kill you," he warned. "They have threatened to kill everyone who comes with messages from the white people. Indians who bring messages are enemies, they say. They tell us this all the time and threaten us with terrible tortures if we side with the white men."

Sarah shrugged off her brother's warning. She had come this far and she was determined not to stop until she had seen her father.

For the first part of the journey, Sarah had been dressed in her usual white woman's clothes. Now she took an Indian blanket out of her saddlebag and began dabbing paint on her face. By the time she was finished, she looked like an authentic squaw.

Lee Winnemucca told his sister that the Bannock encampment was just beyond the next mountain. Knowing the positions of the Bannock lookouts, he told Sarah how to circle the camp and approach it from the north, where the terrain was so rough the Bannocks thought lookouts were unnecessary. Sarah tied her horse to a tree, said good-bye to her brother and her two guides, and started up the trail on foot. It was an agonizing journey. The granite and basalt slopes were so steep that she often had to crawl along on her hands and knees. Knifelike edges of rock cut her palms and fingers and tore at her legs as she struggled across the gouged, eroded slopes. Finally, she found herself on a tree-covered hillside above a mountain lake, looking down on the Bannock camp. It was big. Sarah counted over 300 lodges and close to a thousand warriors.

Hiding in the trees until nightfall, Sarah crept down the hillside into the camp. She quickly located the lodges where the Paiutes were being held. First she pretended to be fussing over some animal skins that had been hung up to dry, then she picked up a load of kindling wood and slipped into her father's lodge. Her paint and blanket confused the Paiutes. It took a few minutes to realize who she was. As soon as they recognized her, they whispered excitedly, "Oh, Sarah, you've come to save us!"

"Perhaps," Sarah said. "First I must talk to my father."

Chief Winnemucca and his daughter sat down in one corner of the lodge to discuss General Howard's message. At first the Chief was reluctant to leave the Bannock camp. "If we are caught," he said, "we will all be killed."

"If you stay here," Sarah reminded him, "the Bannocks will force you to fight with them."

Chief Winnemucca shook his head emphatically. "My people do not want war."

"But if you don't fight, the Bannocks will slaughter you," Sarah said.

Sarah talked with her father for a long time. Several times

during their discussion, Bannock guards came in to check on their prisoners.

In her squaw's costume, Sarah looked just like the other Paiute women, so the Bannocks never realized there was an intruder in their camp. Nor, since they did not understand the Paiute language, could they know what a crucial decision was being made.

Sarah finally convinced Chief Winnemucca that escape was his only choice. "Trust in me," she promised, "I will lead you to safety."

Stealing out of her father's lodge, Sarah made her way down the line of Paiute lodges and hastily whispered instructions to the captives inside. One by one, under cover of the darkness, they crept out of the camp. Seventy-five Paiutes, including Chief Winnemucca, fled along the trail the Bannocks had blazed through the mountains. Around midnight, they were joined by Lee Winnemucca and John and George Paiute, Sarah's guides. They brought with them horses that they had taken from the Bannock herd. The Bannocks had originally stolen them from the Paiutes.

Sarah took charge of the advance party, while her brother Lee and some 20 Paiute braves formed a rear guard. At Sarah's insistence, the fugitives traveled all night. At dawn, after six hours on the trail, they reached a settlement called Summit Springs. Sarah decided it was safe to stop and rest. The Paiutes had barely dismounted when one of Lee Winnemucca's scouts came galloping up to them. "We are followed by the Bannocks!" he cried. "They've fired at our rear guard and they're heading this way."

Remounting their horses, the exhausted Paiutes took off again. If the Bannocks caught up to them, they would never reach Fort Lyon alive. Sarah decided to ride ahead and sound the alarm. Taking her sister-in-law Mattie and John and George Paiute, she set off at a gallop for the army outpost at Sheep Ranch.

General Howard was already at the outpost, anxiously

awaiting Sarah's return. It was about 5:30 in the afternoon of June 14. General Howard was in the office of the former stage station when a sentry shouted, "There's a mounted party in sight!"

A few minutes later, Sarah Winnemucca came galloping into Sheep Ranch, leaped from her horse, and burst into tears. She had ridden 223 miles in three days and two nights, with no sleep and very little to eat or drink. It took Sarah several minutes to regain her composure. When she was finally able to speak, she told General Howard that her father and the other Paiutes were about 20 miles away. She asked him to send a detachment of soldiers to bring them safely back to Fort Lyon.

General Howard went into action, revealing under his gentle manner the toughness and efficiency of the professional soldier. Orders were shouted to the waiting troopers. Bugles blared. Within minutes the cavalry was racing to the rescue of Sarah's father and brother and the rest of the Southern Paiutes. It would have confused John Wayne fans to see those blue-coated troopers thundering down the road to save not a white wagon train but a tribe of Indians in danger of getting killed by other Indians. History is a lot more complicated than Hollywood's version of it.

Once her tribespeople were safe, Sarah gave General Howard a detailed report of the Bannock encampment. She told him how many warriors there were, how many horses they had, the exact location of their camp, and the best way to get to it. Howard soon mounted an expedition against the Bannocks, and the uprising was quelled. Except for one brief flurry of fighting the following year, it was the end of warfare between white men and red men in Idaho.

I wish I could tell you that Sarah Winnemucca and her tribe lived happily ever after. Unfortunately, they did not—but that's another story. I can tell you, however, that through all the Paiutes' subsequent tribulations, Sarah's courage never wavered. She remained their principal champion, and after a six-year struggle, persuaded the United States Senate to pass a special bill granting the land at Malheur to the Southern Paiutes.

Few people know more about courage than a soldier who has commanded men in battle. General Howard never forgot Sarah Winnemucca's heroism in rescuing the Southern Paiutes, nor her long fight to see that her tribe received fair treatment at the hands of the federal government. In his book, *Famous Indian Chiefs I Have Known,* Howard wrote about Sarah Winnemucca.

"If I could tell you but a tenth part of all she willingly did to help the white settlers and her own people to live peaceably together," he declared, "you would think as I do that the name of Thocmetony should have a place beside the name of Pocahontas in the history of our country."

The Middle Sister and the Tree

by Corlia Fourie

In this story drawn from African tales, a young woman must outwit her foes to save her sisters. Some of the unusual words you will encounter in the story are mealies *(corn or millet),* kaross *(a cloak or rug of animal skins), and* marula *(a common tree in the hotter parts of South Africa).*

Once upon a time three sisters lived in a hut in the middle of a great grassy plain. When they shared food or anything else, the eldest and the youngest sisters always knew what they wanted, but the middle sister thought for a long time before making a choice. It took her so long that the other two were already lying on the sleeping mat or had eaten some of the wild figs when she said what she wanted. So long did it take her to decide that her sisters never asked her which games she wanted to play. They simply told her.

But the sisters didn't spend the whole day playing. They also worked. Every day they walked down to the river to fetch water for their mealies.

One morning on the way to the river, the sisters saw a gray wildcat stalking a small bird that was searching for seeds.

128

Just when the wildcat was about to pounce, the three sisters ran and—shoo! shoo!—chased him away.

"Thank you very much," said the little bird, who had only seen the gray wildcat when the sisters had made it run away. "You may each have one wish, and whatever you wish for you'll get. But remember, only one wish each."

"A kaross," the eldest sister said immediately. "I can sleep on it at night and wear it over my shoulders when it's cold."

"I want beads," said the youngest sister. "Beads for my head and my neck and my ears and my arms and my waist and my ankles. Lots and lots of beads!"

The middle sister said nothing. She simply stood there thinking and thinking and thinking.

"What about you?" the little bird asked after a while. "What would you like?"

"It's very difficult," said the middle sister. "Only one wish, and there are so many things I could wish for. I simply don't know yet." Her sisters laughed because they didn't believe the middle sister would ever be able to decide.

But the little bird said, "Think long and hard. I'll be back tomorrow; then you can tell me." And saying so, he flew away.

Early the next morning when the sisters woke up, they saw a kaross and a great many beads in front of the hut.

The eldest and youngest sisters were very pleased.

"How stupid you were," said the eldest sister, "not to choose immediately."

"Yes," said the youngest. She fastened a string of beads around an ankle. "How do you know the little bird will return?"

"He'll come back," said the middle sister. And after she had watered the mealies, she went to sit on a rock to think.

Perhaps she should ask for a new hut because the roof leaked when it rained. No, wait a moment, a larger patch of mealies would be better; then they would be sure of enough food. Or maybe she could wish for the river to be nearer to their home; then they wouldn't have to walk so far for water.

She thought for so long, the sun shifted to the middle of the

129

sky and was burning the crown of her head. "Goodness, but it's hot," she thought. And then she knew what she wanted.

At that moment the little bird came flying up. "Do you know what to wish for by now?" he said.

"I wish there were a big tree near our hut. Then we could sit in its shade when it's hot," said the middle sister.

"That's a good wish," said the little bird, and he flew away.

The middle sister told her sisters about her wish. They all woke up very early the next morning and ran outside. But nothing was there.

The eldest sister said, "That was a really stupid wish. How on earth can a small bird fly here with a large tree in its beak?"

"He told us we could wish for anything," said the middle sister.

Chirp, chirp. They heard bird noises in the tall grass. And when they looked, truly, there was the little bird.

"I pushed the seed into the ground here. Just here." He showed the middle sister. "You must water the seed every day. Then the seed will grow and become a small tree. And the small tree will grow and become a big, a very big tree, indeed."

"What a stupid wish." The youngest sister laughed as she played with her beads. "All your wish has given you is a lot of work."

"You made a good wish," the little bird told the middle sister. "If you do as I've told you, the tree will grow fast. Yes, after three full moons, the tree will be large and strong. It's a marula tree. It will give you much more than shade."

Every day the middle sister fetched water for the seed, and after a few days there was a small tree, which was growing bigger very quickly. Sometimes the girl would stand next to the little tree simply to see it grow. Very soon the tree was so large that she could sit in its shade. And not long after that, the tree was so big that she could climb it. Now the middle sister no longer sat under the tree. No, she sat in the tree.

Her two sisters laughed at her. They laughed because again she was doing the difficult thing. "It's much easier to sit under a tree than in it," they said.

But the middle sister had found a comfortable seat from which she could see clearly through the branches, and nobody could see her from the ground.

One morning after she had finished her tasks, the middle sister climbed into the tree again. She watched the clouds drifting by and the birds flying by . . . and she fell asleep.

She was awakened by angry voices and screams and saw that warriors had captured her sisters! She saw them burning the hut and the mealie patch. She saw the leader hanging the kaross around his own shoulders, and the others sharing the beads among themselves.

When the warriors left with her sobbing sisters, the middle sister also burst into tears.

"Why are you crying?" the little bird asked. He was sitting on a branch just above her head.

"Because I made such a stupid wish," said the middle sister. "If I had waited, I could now wish for my sisters to be free."

"But you made a very good wish," said the little bird. "You have a tree. A marula."

"And of what use is the tree to me now? I have no food. I have no hut to live in. And my sisters are gone." She wept again.

"Look under the tree," said the little bird.

The middle sister looked and saw ripe yellow fruit lying under the tree. She climbed down and ate until her stomach was full.

Then the little bird told her, "Fill a whole pot with fruit and take it to the people who captured your sisters."

The middle sister obeyed the bird. She put the full pot on her head and walked in the direction her sisters had been taken.

Three times she saw the sun jump into the sky, and three times she saw the plains swallowing the sun. Then she reached the village of the people who had captured her sisters.

When the warriors came to capture her as well, she said, "I have brought you a gift." And she took down the pot. She looked into the pot and saw that the fruit had fermented and become a drink.

The warriors tasted. Hmmm. They drank more and more, until they became very drunk and just lay there in the sun, the flies zooming about their heads.

The middle sister ran to the hut where her two sisters were tied with grass ropes. She freed them, and all three went back to the marula tree.

After that day all three sisters lived in the tree. And the tree gave them food. They took turns standing watch and could see the warriors coming a long way off. Then they sat quietly in the tree until the warriors went away again. In this way the tree looked after the sisters for the rest of their lives.

Jimmy Valentine Reforms

by Julia Remine Piggin

Based on a Story by O. Henry

Which takes more courage—to escape from danger—or to risk your own well-being in order to help someone? In this play, Jimmy Valentine has to make that difficult choice.

CHARACTERS

BEN PRICE	DESK CLERK
CRONIN	ANNABEL ADAMS
JIMMY VALENTINE	MR. ADAMS
WARDEN	EMILY
MIKE DOLAN	MAY
BANK MANAGER	AGATHA
BOY	

ACT I

BEN PRICE [*in spotlight, addressing the audience*]: Ever hear of Jimmy Valentine? He was the slickest, smartest, fastest, most skillful safecracker under the sun. He used the best set of safecracking tools ever invented. Drills, punches, bits, clamps, augers, and some that nobody had ever seen before, because he'd

133

dreamed them up himself. They'd been specially made for him, and cost as much as most of us make in a year, but Jimmy soon got it back. It took him minutes to drill open the toughest safe in any town he passed through. And I am Ben Price, the detective who tracked him down, and caught him, and struggled with him, and brought him in, and gave the evidence that got him a four-year prison sentence. I was a hero for a while. But 10 months later....

[*He shrugs and exits. Lights go up in the prison shoe shop.* JIMMY VALENTINE *sits on a bench, stitching the upper of a leather shoe. He is a handsome young man, even in the striped convict uniform of the 1890s, but he looks bored and tired.* CRONIN, *a guard, enters the shop and walks over to* JIMMY.]

CRONIN: On your feet, Valentine. The Warden wants to see you.

JIMMY: What's the Warden want with me?

CRONIN: I don't ask *him* questions, you don't ask *me* questions. Come on, he's waiting for you.

JIMMY: Okay, okay, keep your corset on.

[*He rises, puts down the shoe.* CRONIN *gives him a push toward the door. Lights go up in the* WARDEN'S *office. The* WARDEN *sits at his desk, studying a piece of paper. There is a knock at the door.*]

CRONIN: Cronin, with prisoner 9762.

WARDEN: Bring him in. [CRONIN *brings* JIMMY *into the office.*]

CRONIN: Here he is, Warden.

WARDEN: So I see. Well, Valentine, your friends didn't forget you.

JIMMY: Whatever do you mean, sir?

WARDEN: You know perfectly well what I mean. You expected it a lot sooner than ten months, didn't you? But it came through. The governor signed your pardon this morning.

CRONIN: He was supposed to serve four years!

WARDEN: He has the right friends in the right places. Find him some street clothes, Cronin, and call him at seven tomorrow morning. You'll report to the bull pen, Valentine, and get your going-away money and your train ticket and your cigar, and go your merry way. But listen, just a piece of advice. Why not try going straight this time? You're a bright guy—you can get an honest job. Find out what's it's like to *earn* your money for a change. Forget about safecracking.

JIMMY: Why, whatever can you mean? I never cracked a safe in my life! [CRONIN *snorts.*]

WARDEN: Cut it, Valentine. What about the job in Springfield that got you in here? That mean old jury just didn't like your looks, I suppose.

JIMMY: You are exactly right. I have never been to Springfield in my life.

WARDEN: Take him away, Cronin. [CRONIN *takes* JIMMY'S *arm, starts for the door.*] I don't know where you're going tomorrow, Valentine, but think over what I said.

[BEN PRICE *walks into the spotlight again.*]

BEN: Maybe the Warden didn't know where Jimmy was going, but I did. I knew him. After a few sniffs of fresh air, he would head to a good restaurant for a chicken cooked the way they don't do them in prison kitchens, a bottle of wine, and a better cigar than they gave him in the bull pen. Then, three hours on a train to a little town near the state line, and then a short walk to a café owned by Mike Dolan. That's where Mr. Valentine and I had our last meeting. I lost a shirt button in the fight—and he lost ten months of his freedom.

[*He walks off and the lights go up inside* MIKE DOLAN'S *café.* MIKE *is leaning on the bar, reading a newspaper.* JIMMY *comes in, dressed in a bright-colored, ill-fitting suit.*]

JIMMY: Morning, partner.

MIKE: Jimmy Valentine! [*He runs from around the bar, embraces* JIMMY.] You're a sight for sore eyes! Jimmy, I'm sorry we couldn't get you out any sooner, but the people in Springfield kept making these protests. Letters to the paper, picketing with signs. The governor nearly said no at the last minute. Are you all right? That suit they gave you ain't exactly your style.

JIMMY: No, but it's not permanent. Got my key?

MIKE: Right here. [*He reaches behind him, takes a key off a*

135

board, and gives it to JIMMY.] Pretty dusty in there. Nobody's been in your room since that detective dragged you out.

JIMMY: See you later. [*He goes to the back of the café and unlocks a door. Lights go up on a sparsely furnished room.* JIMMY *bends down, picks up a button from the floor, and laughs.*] Button, button, who's got Ben Price's button? [*He flips the button into the air, pulls a bed away from the wall, slides open a wall panel, and pulls out a dust-covered suitcase. He snaps it open and gazes at the set of gleaming burglar tools inside. He leans down and kisses the tools.*] Babies, you waited for me! You won't be sorry. Just let me change my clothes and we'll go out on the town.

> [*Lights go up in the café as* JIMMY *comes from the back, dressed in a handsome, perfectly fitted suit, carrying his cleaned-off suitcase.*]

MIKE: Hey, you look a lot better in your own duds. [*Indicates suitcase.*] Got any plans for your friends there?

JIMMY: Why, whatever can you mean? I'm the sales representative for the New York Amalgamated Short Snap Biscuit Cracker and Frazzled Wheat Company. [MIKE *doubles over with laughter.*] Thanks for everything, friend. I won't write, but keep reading that paper.

> [*He exits.* BEN PRICE *comes back into the spotlight.*]

BEN: I knew it wouldn't be long. A week after Valentine, Number 9762, was out, there was a neat job of safe burglary in Richmond, Indiana. Not a witness, not a clue. Only got 800 bucks that time, but there were happier days ahead. Two weeks later an absolutely guaranteed burglarproof safe in Logansport was opened like peeling a cheese. Only cash was taken, cash that couldn't be traced, to the tune of 10,000 dollars. And then an old-fashioned bank safe in Jefferson City turned into a volcano and threw 12,000 dollars in bank notes out of its crater. That's when they called me in.

> [*The Jefferson City* BANK MANAGER *joins* BEN.]

BANK MANAGER: Detective Price, do you have any idea who could have done this to my bank?

BEN: I know who did it. There's only one safecracker in America who could have. Only one with the tools and the know-how. Jimmy Valentine. Look, I'm going after him, and this time he won't get out in a few months. But it's going to take a while. He knows how to crack a safe, and he knows how to hide.

> [*We move to the main street of Elmore, Arkansas, a small-town business district. Storefronts flank a door under a sign reading "Elmore Bank." Another sign reads "Planters Hotel."* JIMMY VALENTINE, *looking handsome in an expensive suit, carrying his suitcase, appears at the end of the street and walks the length of it, observing. As he comes to the bank, the door opens and* ANNABEL ADAMS, *pretty and beautifully dressed, comes out.* JIMMY *almost bumps into her, stands back, and stares at her. He is obviously smitten.* ANNABEL *is flustered, embarrassed by his stare but plainly pleased. She smiles nervously, walks a few steps down the street, and then turns, looks back at* JIMMY, *turns again, and hurries away. A little boy is hanging around the door of the bank.* JIMMY *speaks to him.*]

JIMMY: Hey, kid, isn't that Miss Polly Smithers? I think I was in school with her.

BOY: No, 'course not, that's Annabel Adams. Everybody knows that. She's the prettiest lady in town. And she's rich, too. Her pa owns the bank.

JIMMY: Annabel, huh? [*He repeats the name lovingly.*] Annabel. One more thing, kid—where's the best hotel in town?

BOY: There's only one hotel, and it's right down the street. [*He points.*] Everybody knows that.

JIMMY: I'm new in town. [*He digs out a dime and gives it to the boy.*] Thanks.

> [*He leans out, looks in the direction* ANNABEL *went, and then turns and walks to the hotel. He goes into the lobby. The* DESK CLERK *looks at his big-city clothes and smiles broadly.*]

DESK CLERK: May I help you, sir?

JIMMY: Yes, I need a room. But first, do you have a good shoe store in this town?

DESK CLERK: Well, no, not a real shoe store. The general stores and the drygoods stores sell some, mostly work boots and sandals, but for good shoes we have to go into Little Rock or order from a catalog. Why? You need a new pair of shoes?

JIMMY: No, no, shoes are my line. I know all about shoes. [*He smiles at the memory of how he learned.*] Frankly, I've been looking for a town to settle down in and maybe open a shoe store. This looks like a good little place. Reminds me of the town I grew up in.

DESK CLERK: Well, we like it. Might be a little quiet for a man like you. We don't have the kind of tailor shops you buy your suits at.

JIMMY: I don't think I'd find it too dull. You've got some very nice-looking people here. Very nice-looking. I think I'll stay a while and see if I can get to know them. How about that room?

DESK CLERK [*reaching back for a key*]: The best room in the hotel. Can I call the bellhop to help you with your suitcase?

JIMMY: No, no, it's got some—uh—samples in it. I like to carry it myself. [*He starts toward the stairs.*]

DESK CLERK: Sir, I'm sorry—you didn't register.

JIMMY: Oh, of course.

[*He walks back to the desk and signs in. The* DESK CLERK *turns the register around.*]

DESK CLERK: Mr. Ralph Spencer. Enjoy your stay, Mr. Spencer. We're glad to have you with us.

[BEN PRICE *comes back to the spotlight.*]

BEN: Jimmy knew how to disappear. In the past, I'd tracked him from the jobs he pulled. But now, the jobs stopped. For more than a year, there wasn't a burglary anywhere that Jimmy Valentine wouldn't have been ashamed to have his name on. Dynamite, smashed doors, sloppy—not his style. Then I got a tip about a handsome young man who had opened a shoe store in an Arkansas town. He'd made a bang-up success of it, charmed the town's leading families, and was engaged to be married to the daughter of the owner of the bank. Some of it seemed to fit. Some of it didn't make much sense. Jimmy had stolen a bundle in those robberies he pulled before I lost him. Enough to set up a whole new life. But why would he want to? I had to check it out. I didn't learn until a long time later, on another case, about a letter "Mr. Spencer" wrote a few days before I got to Elmore. It was a letter that made an appointment. And that appointment changed all of our lives.

[*Lights pick up* JIMMY *at a desk in the hotel lobby. He is writing.*]

JIMMY [*reading as he writes*]: Dear Billy: I want you to meet me at Sullivan's in Little Rock, next Wednesday night at nine o'clock. It's important. I want you to wind up some things for me, and to give you a present. My kit of tools. You couldn't get a set like it for several thousand dollars, and I will never need them again. I quit the old business, Billy, more than a year ago. I own a fine store, and I'm making a good and honest living. And two weeks from now, I'm going to marry the best and most beautiful young woman on earth. She's an angel. She believes in me. I would never do another crooked thing for the whole world. After we're married I plan to sell out and move out West. There won't be as much danger of having old scores brought up against me there. Be sure to be at Sully's. Your old friend, Jimmy Valentine.

[*Lights dim and go up on* BEN.]

BEN: I got into Elmore on that Wednesday morning. Came on an early train, so I had time to nose around a little. I found a little place to have breakfast across from Spencer's Shoe Store, which wasn't all that far from the bank and the hotel. [*A sign has been added to the others on Main Street.*] I was finishing my coffee when the whole Adams family gathered in front of the bank. My waitress told me who they were. There was Mr. Adams, the kingpin of the bank, and there was Annabel, who sure lived up to her title of prettiest lady in town. I felt kind of sorry for her, for she was holding on to the arm of—Jimmy Valentine. [*As he talks, the people he mentions appear.*] And

139

there was Emily, Annabel's married sister, and her two little girls, Agatha, who looked about five, and May, who must have been about nine. Jimmy said something to Annabel, and dashed down the street to the hotel, where he still lived. He came back in a few minutes, carrying that famous suitcase. Their voices drifted over to me across the street, and I could hear them chattering about seeing the new vault in the bank. The whole bunch of them went into the bank. I paid my check and went over. I didn't plan to come out alone.

[*Everyone moves inside the bank.* JIMMY *sets down his suitcase.*]

ANNABEL: Papa, don't forget, Ralph has ordered a buggy to take him to the station, so we don't have too much time. He's going to Little Rock to order his wedding suit. [*She takes* JIMMY'S *hat off his head and puts it on her own, and then picks up the suitcase.*] Wouldn't I make a good salesman? Ralph, this suitcase is so heavy. It feels as if it's full of bricks.

JIMMY: Nickel-plated shoehorns. They sent me about 10 times too many and I thought I'd return them myself and save express charges. I'm getting awfully economical now I'm going to be a married man.

[ANNABEL *puts her arm around his waist. They look at each other adoringly.*]

MR. ADAMS: All right, let's not waste any more valuable time. Come back here and see my pride and joy. [*The party follows him to the rear of the bank, where the vault stands, its heavy door open.*] There she is. Latest model made. [*He turns the bolts and the handle of the door.*] It fastens with three solid steel bolts thrown at the same second with a single handle. And it has a time lock. Look, Ralph, I know safes don't interest you very much, but it's a new design, patented. Has a time lock. Look inside—isn't that a beauty? Come around here to the back, see how it's finished.

[*The adults follow him to the back, behind the vault. The children go on playing with the clock and knobs on the door. There is a loud clanging sound.* BEN PRICE *walks into the bank and stands near the front door, as* EMILY *screams.*]

EMILY: Agatha! Where's Agatha? May, where's your sister?

MAY: She wanted to go inside! She went in and I shut the door. [*The vault door is closed.*]

ADAMS: Did you turn anything? Did you touch the bolts?

MAY: I just did what you did, only after I shut the door [*Inside the vault* AGATHA *begins to scream for her mother.*]

AGATHA: Mama, mama, get me out! I'm scared!

ADAMS [*tugging at the handle*]**:** The door can't be opened. The clock wasn't wound. The combination wasn't set.

EMILY: Get her out! You've got to get her out!

[AGATHA *goes on screaming.* MAY *begins to cry loudly.*]

ADAMS: Please, please, let's try to be calm.

EMILY: Open it, open it! Oh, my baby! She'll die of fright! Oh, please, Papa—Ralph—do something!

ADAMS: My God, Spencer, what shall we do? There isn't a man nearer than Little Rock who can open that door. The child can't stand it for long in there. There isn't enough air, even if she doesn't die of fright.

ANNABEL: Oh, Ralph, please! Isn't there anything you can do? [JIMMY *stands perfectly still and looks at* ANNABEL. *There is a strange smile on his lips. He knows the choice he must make. He takes a deep breath.*]

JIMMY: Annabel, give me that rosebud you're wearing on your dress.

ANNABEL [*bewildered*]**:** What?

[*But she unpins the rosebud and puts it in* JIMMY'S *hand.* JIMMY *looks at it and slips it into his vest pocket. Then he throws off his coat and rolls up his shirtsleeves.*]

JIMMY: Stand back, all of you. [*He picks up the suitcase, looks around, and sets it on a table near the vault. He opens it. Everyone gasps as they see the gleaming burglar tools.* JIMMY *begins to take them out, one by one, and lines them up on the* *table. He studies them for a moment. He selects a drill, fits it to the proper handle, and calls into the vault.*] Agatha, get back from the door. Do as I say.

> [*He lifts the drill and places it against the door. It bites into the steel. The sound of drilling fills the room. Everyone watches, as if under a spell.* JIMMY *breaks his own record. In minutes, he throws back the bolts and opens the door.* AGATHA *runs out into her mother's arms.*]

AGATHA: Mama, mama!

EMILY: My baby!

ANNABEL [*taking a step toward* JIMMY]*:* Ralph—

> [JIMMY *does not look at her. He grabs his coat, puts it on, and strides to the front door where* BEN PRICE *is standing.*]

JIMMY: Ben. So you got here at last. Well, let's go. It doesn't really make much of a difference now.

BEN [*hesitating a second*]*:* I think you've made a mistake, Mr. Spencer. I don't believe I recognize you. There's a buggy waiting out there? Is it for you? [JIMMY *stands frozen as* BEN *turns and walks down the street. At the far end he turns to the audience.*] And that was the last time I ever saw Jimmy Valentine.

Welcome

by David Hernandez

When I was little and brown
The humming plane stopped
Midway Field was there
And I was proud of my blue shorts
White shirt
Blue socks
White shoes
True Puerto
Rican proud.
Excited by Colgate smiles
Like the ads nailed
To my town's walls.
So I was confused
And shivered
When the December
Chicago wind
Slapped my face.

The Babysitter

by Gary Soto

What is the line between being brave and being reckless? Gary Soto tells about learning the difference, in this true account of a day when he was 12.

hen Frank, our babysitter from juvie, picked some black stuff from under his fingernail with a playing card and suggested that we take my mom's car (Mom was out dancing for the evening), I stopped marching around the living room with smashed Pepsi cans on the heels of my tennis shoes. I had never been in a car driven by someone who was only three years older than me, which is to say, a 15-year-old. Rick, my older brother, was camping in a friend's backyard, while Debra played on the couch with our baby brother.

"You don't know how to drive," I said, unhooking the Pepsi cans from my shoes. But I was eager to help drive the car. I had once started the car and revved it up until smoke filled the garage and the five kids sitting with me became sick. The mother of one of the other kids later called, and I was spanked from one corner of the room to the other. I thought of that day and shook my head. "Mom'll find out."

Frank fanned out a deck of cards on the kitchen table and asked, "How?"

"She just will."

He shuffled the cards and said, "Pick one."

I picked a card: a jack of clubs with a little spittle of plum on his chin. He reshuffled the deck, fanned out the cards again, and said, "Pick another."

It was the jack, with the glob of plum.

Frank got up from the table and dipped his pudgy fingers into the Disneyland coffee cup where the keys were kept. "Come on, don't be a baby." My baby brother looked up with spittle from thumb sucking hanging on his face. Debra got off the couch. "Mom's gonna get you if you drive her car."

"No, sir," I said. I looked up at Frank. "Will she?"

Frank said we could go for a short ride, and if we didn't tell he would buy us a milkshake. He said he was almost 15, and on farms people knew how to drive tractors when they were 12. I said he didn't live on a farm, but he said that I was missing the point. He reminded us that he would buy us a shake, a jumbo one if we agreed. Debra looked at me, and I at her. That was enough for us, and we carried the baby into our Chevy, which was parked in the driveway. While we snuck into the car, ever mindful of the neighbors, Frank walked tall as a Marine and twirled the keychain on his index finger.

"Stay down," I warned Debra and my baby brother, who were in the backseat on their knees. Frank started the engine, adjusted the mirror and the seat, and said, "Here goes," not looking over his shoulder as he backed out of the driveway. I peeked out of the window like an alligator and saw Cross-Eyed Johnny shooting marbles in his driveway. A shirtless Mr. Prince was watering his yellow lawn. Mrs. Hancock was tying back a rose bush with strips of bedsheet.

The Chevy purred as it picked up speed, a tail of blue smoke trailing. When the car slowed to a stop at the end of the block, we sat up. Frank seemed in control. He looked both ways, then accelerated smoothly, warm wind filling the car and rattling the newspapers on the floorboard.

As we drove up a street past neighbors sitting in lawn chairs under the orange glow of porch lights, Debra said she wanted a banana shake. I thought chocolate would be fine, though banana would be okay as long as we had two straws to pump our cheeks full of sweetness. Our baby brother, who had yet to squeal more than "Mama" and "shasha," said nothing. He was pulling at the thread of a busted seam in the upholstery.

I noticed one of Frank's arms cocked on the window. I told him he had better drive with both hands, but he laughed and said driving was safer with one hand because the other hand was needed to signal for turns. He slouched down, and I said he should sit up so he could see more of the road. He laughed and said slouching was safer because if we got in a wreck his face wouldn't hit the windshield. Debra asked if we were going to get in a wreck, and he said, "Only if we stop." He ran a stop sign and laughed so that spittle flew from his mouth. It was then that I knew we had made a mistake getting in the car with him. He laughed and looked at us with his eyes closed. He laughed and wriggled the steering wheel so that the car shimmied. He laughed and took both hands off the wheel. He laughed when the car veered toward the gutter and leaves exploded into the air. I socked him in the arm, hard, and told him he had better drive right, or else.

Frank's laughter wound down to a giggle. "Okay," he said. He turned onto Belmont Avenue and as we approached the Starlight burger stand, he said, "Is that where you want to get your milkshakes?"

"Yeah, that's it," we screamed. Our baby brother got up on his knees to look. A silvery thread hung from his wet mouth.

The car got closer and closer, and Frank repeated, "Is that it, that one?"

"Yeah," we screamed again.

"That one," he repeated, "that one?"

Yeah, yeah, yeah.

Frank laughed and passed up the burger stand. "Oops, we missed it."

We sat back down, feeling cheated. The air about us stank of burgers.

Frank made a reckless U-turn that made the tires squeal, and our baby brother rolled over like a sack of groceries. I socked Frank in the arm and warned him that he had better drive right. He said "Okay, okay, all right already." He smirked, then smiled a large, idiot grin as we approached the burger stand we had just passed. He pointed again and asked: "That one?"

Debra and I leaned our faces into the open window, warm air gushing into our mouths. "Yeah, that one."

"That one?" Frank kidded.

"Yeah, that one," we screamed a little louder.

The Chevy slowed but didn't stop. I saw a kid about my age, cheeks collapsed, sucking on a milkshake, and a baby in a stroller feeding on a spoonful of ice cream. At a redwood table, a family of four was biting into their burgers at the same time. Mad, I climbed into the backseat. Debra and I grumbled and crossed our arms. Our baby brother played with strings of his spittle. He smiled at me, and I could see real string looped on the back of his mouth. Grimacing, I scraped his tongue of string and a milky paste.

I turned to Frank. "You're a liar," I said, trying to hurt his feelings. "You were a liar before you were born!"

Frank laughed and said, "No, the car just didn't stop. I think something's wrong with the brakes." He scared his face into lines and bugged out his eyes. He shielded his face with his arms and screamed, "Look out! Look out!" as we came to a red light. The Chevy groaned to a halt, and he turned around, with one arm on the seat, and said, "I guess the brakes fixed themselves."

Frank punched the gas pedal and the Chevy coughed and jerked forward while our heads jerked back. Baby brother rolled over one more time, fingers in his mouth.

"We wanna get out, right now!" I said. "I mean it!"

"I'm going to tell Mom," Debra threatened.

Frank looked into the rear view mirror with closed eyes. "Wanna get out? Good idea." He opened the door and stuck one foot out. I saw the rush of asphalt, some burger stand litter, and one poor sparrow flattened to an oily shadow.

"You better drive us back home, right now," Debra said. "I mean it!"

"Right now? No, we're gonna get a milkshake." He closed the door and did a U-turn. We looked ahead: the burger stand's neon was fluttering, saying BU G RS FOR YO. There were two cars and people ordering under a stinky fan. Music was blaring from a loudspeaker.

We began to smell burgers, and I could hear the slurp of a drained Coke. Frank pointed and asked, "That one? That one right there?"

We looked but didn't say anything. I was wondering if Rick and I could beat him up. Debra could help out, and maybe we could pin him to the floor and let baby brother drool on his face. Maybe when we got home Mom would be standing in the front window with a belt in her hands. I figured that Frank would get the first spanking, and then Mom would be too tired to spank us that hard. She might not even spank us at all, only make us do the dishes until we moved out of the house.

Only after baby brother messed his plastic pants, and Debra and I yanked together on Frank's hair so that a muscle in his neck popped, did we return to our street and the sound of hissing sprinklers in the summer dark. We slammed the car door, cussed, and stomped into the house with a smirking Frank offering apologies. We changed baby brother, who squealed and bit more holes into his rubber rattler. Debra and I picked up a bundle of crayons and sat down at the kitchen table. Frank shuffled the cards, played game after game of solitaire, cheating each time, and then asked as he got up to fix a pitcher of purple Kool-Aid, "Whatta you guys wanna do?"

Why Brer Possum Has No Hair on His Tail

by Julius Lester

Africans, brought to North America as slaves, told stories that proved the power of quick wits over brute force. Brer Rabbit is often the trickster in these stories. Many were collected as "Uncle Remus" stories by a journalist from Georgia, Joel Chandler Harris. They have been retold by other writers as well. In this story, desperation makes for a special sort of courage. When Brer Possum finds himself in trouble, there's nothing he won't do to get out of it.

There aren't too many tales about Brer Possum. That's because he never did that much. Why would he? Brer Possum is one of the laziest animals in creation. One time, though, his laziness got him in trouble.

On this particular day Brer Possum woke up hungry. If you and I wake up hungry, we go to the refrigerator, get a slice of cold pizza, and tell our stomachs that it is time to go to work. Brer Possum woke up hungry and did not know what to do. He hung there in the tree, upside down, his tail curled around a limb, listening to his stomach. His stomach was saying, "Fool! Go find some cold pizza!"

Brer Possum was too lazy to go anywhere. He thought if he hung there long enough, food would come to him. He changed his mind, however, when he overheard his stomach tell Ol' Man

Death, "Come get this fool!" Brer Possum decided it was time to do something.

He dropped out of the tree at the very minute Brer Rabbit was walking by, and almost landed on him.

"You trying to hit me?" Brer Rabbit hollered angrily.

"No, no, Brer Rabbit. Why would I do that? You and me always been the best of friends."

"That's true," Brer Rabbit agreed. "So tell me. How you be?"

"I'm hungry," said Brer Possum.

"A body has to be smart to keep a full stomach these days," Brer Rabbit agreed. "But I believe I know where you can get as much to eat as you want."

"Where's that?" Brer Possum asked eagerly.

"Brer Bear's apple orchard. Brer Bear don't care nothing about apples. He's a honey man. He watches the bees when they come to the apple blossoms. When the bees leave he follows them to their hive and gets the honey."

Brer Possum lit out for Brer Bear's apple orchard. Sure enough, the trees were full of the reddest, juiciest apples you can imagine. Brer Possum climbed to the top of the biggest tree and proceeded to do away with some apples.

While Brer Possum was getting fat on the apples, what do you think Brer Rabbit was doing? He was banging on Brer Bear's door.

"Brer Bear! Brer Bear! There's somebody in your apple trees."

Brer Bear came barreling out of the house. He couldn't afford to have somebody eating his apples. That's what he filled up on before he went into hibernation every winter. He lit out for the apple orchard.

Brer Possum thought he heard somebody coming. "Just one more apple."

He ate another one. He heard something again, and it was closer this time.

"Just one more."

The noise was closer now. Brer Possum looked out over the

landscape and there was Brer Bear running toward the orchard like a runaway horse.

"Just one more," said Brer Possum.

That was one more too many.

Brer Possum was still chewing when Brer Bear started shaking the tree with all his strength, and down came Brer Possum like a leaf in a November wind.

But Brer Possum's feet were moving before he touched the ground, and when he did, those little legs shot him five feet down the road.

Brer Bear took off after him. Brer Bear may be big but he ain't slow. Uh-uh. It wasn't long before Brer Bear caught up to Brer Possum and grabbed him.

That didn't mean a thing to Brer Possum. Caught or not, Brer Possum didn't stop moving his legs. They were churning and turning and kicking up grass so bad that Brer Bear's grip was slipping. He bent over and grabbed Brer Possum's tail in his teeth.

That didn't slow Brer Possum down either. His little legs were still flinging dirt and grass back into Brer Bear's eyes. Brer Possum kicked and scratched and scratched and kicked until you would have thought a little tornado had landed. He kicked and scratched until he kicked and scratched his tail right out of Brer Bear's teeth. And all the hair on his tail came off in Brer Bear's mouth.

Brer Bear started coughing and gagging and he might've strangulated to death if Brer Rabbit hadn't come along and beat him on the back until Brer Possum's hair came out of his throat.

The hair may have come out of Brer Bear's throat, but it didn't go back on Brer Possum's tail. That's why, from that day to this, the Possum has no hair on his tail.

Start Your Own Successful Business

by Debbi Fields

What does it take to begin a new venture? Launching a business is a lot like moving to a new place, with frightening uncertainties and the hope of success. Here's advice—including a cookie recipe—from the founder of Mrs. Fields' Cookies.

As a little girl, I didn't know that I would go into the cookie business, but there was always a guiding force: I knew that whatever I did, it would be something where I could watch people smile. I began baking when I was 13 years old, and whenever someone took a bite of one of my cookies, I saw a big smile on their face.

When I was 20, I decided it was time to think about what I wanted to do for the rest of my life. My father had always told me, "Do something you love." For me, that was baking cookies. As I built up Mrs. Fields' Cookies, I learned some secrets for starting a successful business. They can help whether you're starting a lemonade stand, a dog-walking service, or some bigger business venture.

Choose something you love to do. By focusing on something you really enjoy, you're much more likely to succeed. It should be something that you'd spend your free time doing anyway. Because I loved to bake all the time, my cookies got better and better. This success made me enjoy baking even more. One reinforced the other.

The greatest failure is not to try. Even though I had no business experience, I decided to open the first Mrs. Fields' Cookies store about 16 years ago. Everyone I encountered said things like, "Oh, you can't do that. You'll fail. That's a stupid idea. Don't try." People don't like to venture into the unknown. But trying an unknown enterprise means that you're getting ready to learn something new.

I kept reminding myself that the greatest failure was not to try. And even if I didn't succeed, trying would be better than doing nothing.

Try anything . . . and everything. After my store was open, I waited for customers to come and buy my cookies. And I waited . . . and waited. Hours passed, but nobody came into my store. It was depressing! It looked as though what everybody had told me was true: I was unsuccessful, nobody would buy my cookies, I was going to fail. So I said to myself, "Well, I can't just sit here and watch this happen. I have to try something. Not trying is simply asking for failure."

That's when I took a sheet of cookies and marched up and down the street, stopping people and offering them samples. Some of them came back to my store and bought cookies—and the rest, as they say, is history. What did the trick is the unconventional wisdom that if one thing doesn't work, you have to keep trying new ideas until something does stick. You never want to close the book on your dreams and think, "Oh, if only I had tried this, or done that!" Try everything. Sure, you might fail; maybe it just wasn't meant to be. But at least you'll know in your heart of hearts that you gave it your very best shot.

Don't go into business just to make money. I've heard lots of people say, "I want to make a million dollars." They go into business only for money, rather than to provide a product or service they absolutely love. This is a mistake. Unless they find something they're passionate about, they'll never make it.

In life you have to understand what's most valuable. When I was growing up, my father used to say to me, "True wealth is family and friends." He was right.

After you've got your business started, follow these guidelines for running it successfully.

Don't ask anyone to do something you wouldn't do yourself. Be willing to do the hardest jobs, the ones nobody else wants. In my business it might be something like mopping the floors or putting things away. Once I went into one of my stores in San Diego, California, and the supplies had just arrived—sacks of flour, chocolate chips, butter, and so forth. The first thing I did was start putting it away. The employees said, "Stop, Debbi; don't *you* do that!" I said, "No, come on; we're a team." I'm a real believer that you create teams by working *together.* My success didn't come because of Debbi Fields, but because the people I worked with allowed me to succeed.

Look at your mistakes as chances to learn. Some of my biggest mistakes have also been the most educational. As an example, one day the state of California came to me and said I was violating state regulations by having 18-year-olds clean the mixers in my stores. The state levied a heavy fine. I didn't know how I'd ever find the money to pay it. I went to see the judge, who said, "I understand that you didn't know the regulations, but that doesn't excuse you." Right then, I realized that you need to spend time learning every aspect of your business. You can't afford to be ignorant. Getting my hand slapped taught me a valuable lesson, and it's a good thing it happened when I had only a few stores. What if it had happened when I had 700 stores? I'd probably have been fined right out of business.

It's amazing but true that some things you think are horrible actually end up to be a blessing. I've always believed that life teaches us in a way that sometimes looks like a negative, but generally always turns out to be a positive.

There may come a time when you want to expand your business—open a second store, add employees, buy more equipment, and so forth. Here are a few guidelines.

"No" is not an acceptable answer when seeking financing. "Financing" is the money needed to start or expand a business, and it's actually obtained from a bank. When I was starting out, I went to bank after bank. They'd listen to my plans (and eat all the cookies I brought) and then say no. I told myself, "I know there's somebody out there who wants to say yes. I just have to find them!" That gave me the courage to keep knocking on doors, even when people shut the doors in my face. I couldn't stop because the day I stopped searching meant that my dream would never be realized. I just don't believe in giving up.

You must have command of your business. A lot of people want to expand, but they don't have their first business running steadily yet. In particular, you need to know all the costs involved in your business, because they're going to multiply as you grow.

Find enthusiastic employees. Surround yourself with people who love the product or service as much as you do. Let's say you have a dog-grooming business. Find people who *love* dogs and enjoy taking care of them.

Provide excellent training. I think that training should go on every day, and I've always viewed myself as a teacher. I never say to someone, "Do this." Instead, I explain *why.* For instance, our stores never sell a cookie that's more than two hours out of the oven. (The resulting "cookie orphans" are donated to charity.) It's not that the cookies self-destruct after two hours or taste awful. It's just that I always want to have fresh cookies coming out of the oven, because the most important thing we offer is the experience that a warm cookie creates. When I ask employees what happens when they serve a warm cookie, they tell me, "The customer says 'Mmmmm!'" The employees realize that the two-hour limit isn't just a silly rule, but part of a philosophy of doing business.

Actually, I don't see myself as being in the cookie business. My job is to generate a smile, and it just happens to come in the form of a cookie. I hope *you* will find a way to spread smiles in your life and business, too.

Krispie Kandy Bar Cookies from
Mrs. Fields' Kitchen

Ingredients

2 cups all-purpose flour

1 cup quick oats (not instant)

1 teaspoon baking soda

¼ teaspoon salt

¾ cup brown sugar

¾ cup granulated sugar

1 cup butter (2 sticks) softened to room temperature (do not microwave)

2 eggs

2 teaspoons pure vanilla extract

10- to 12-ounce crispy-rice chocolate bar (broken into ½-inch chunks)

How to bake them:

Preheat oven to 300 degrees.

In a medium bowl, mix together the flour, oats, baking soda, and salt with a wire whisk. Set aside. With an electric mixer on medium speed, blend both sugars together in a large, deep bowl until they're the consistency of fluffy sand. Cut each stick of butter into four pieces and beat together with the sugars until creamy. Scrape down the sides of the bowl with a rubber spatula.

Add the eggs and vanilla, and beat on low speed until the mixture is fully blended. Add the flour-oat mixture and candy bar chunks. Mix on low speed until just blended. Do not overmix.

Form the cookies with a 1½-ounce ice cream scoop, or use a rounded tablespoon. Drop them onto an ungreased cookie sheet, spacing them 2 inches apart. Bake in the oven for 20-22 minutes. They are done when the edges turn golden and the cookies spring back when touched. Don't brown them. Immediately transfer the cookies to a cool surface.

Yields: 30 three-inch cookies.

Mrs. Fields' Baking "Doughs and Don'ts"

Making the dough

■ Do start with the freshest, purest ingredients available—fresh butter, real vanilla extract, nothing artificial or imitation.

■ Don't use a microwave to melt your butter or margarine, because this creates dark, flat, greasy cookies. Just allow the butter or margarine to warm up to room temperature.

■ Don't overmix the dough, which can make it runny and produce tough cookies. If the dough is too soft, chill it in the refrigerator for 20 minutes.

Baking

■ Don't use dark pans, which tend to burn the bottoms of cookies. Instead, use shiny aluminum cookie sheets.

■ Do drop cookie dough with an ice cream scoop to make perfectly sized and shaped cookies.

■ Do cool the cookie sheets before dropping cookies, to prevent spreading.

■ Do use the "touch" method to know when your cookies are finished baking. If the cookie has spring to it, similar to cake, the cookie is perfect.

Cooling and storing

■ Do immediately transfer cookies from the cookie sheet to a cool surface.

■ Don't place cookies on a chopping block to cool. They may pick up the flavor of garlic or onion you chopped for last night's dinner.

■ Do store cookies in an airtight container with a piece of bread (which helps the cookies stay soft).

■ Don't refrigerate cookies. Freeze them in an airtight bag while they're still fresh and reheat or thaw at room temperature when you're ready to eat them.

(Acknowldgements continued from page 2)

"74th Street" is from *The Malibu and Other Poems* by Myra Cohn Livingston. Copyright © 1972 Myra Cohn Livingston. Reprinted by permission of Marian Reiner for the author.

"Zlateh the Goat" text copyright © 1966 by Isaac Bashevis Singer.

"Gator Aid" from *Library of Curious and Unusual Facts:Above and Beyond* by the Editors of Time-Life Books © 1992 Time-Life Books Inc.

"In White Tie" is excerpted from "Going: 1960-1970" from *Paper Boy* by David Huddle, © 1979. Reprinted by permission of the University of Pittsburgh Press.

From *The Hundred Penny Box* by Sharon Bell Mathis. Copyright © 1975 by Sharon Bell Mathis, text. Used by permission of Viking Penguin, a division of Penguin Books USA Inc.

"Mother to Son" from *Selected Poems* by Langston Hughes. Copyright 1926 by Alfred A. Knopf, Inc. and renewed 1954 by Langston Hughes. Reprinted by permission of the publisher.

"Li Chi Slays the Serpent" from *Chinese Fairy Tales and Fantasies* by Moss Roberts, translator and editor. Copyright © 1979 by Moss Roberts. Reprinted by permission of Pantheon Books, a division of Random House, Inc.

"Flight into Danger" by Arthur Hailey © 1956 from *Ten Canadian Plays* published by Dell © 1975.

"You've Got To Be Kidding" from *Dave Barry Is Not Making This Up* by Dave Barry. Copyright © 1994 by Dave Barry. Reprinted by permission of Crown Publishers, Inc.

"Beware: Do Not Read this Poem" © 1968 by Ishmael Reed from *Cathechism of a Neo-American Hoodoo Church.* Reprinted by permission.

"Lament" by Edna St. Vincent Millay. From *Collected Poems,* HarperCollins. © 1921, 1948 by Edna St. Vincent Millay. Reprinted by permission of Elizabeth Barnett, literary executor.

"Thurgood Marshall: Fight for Justice." Copyright © 1993 Troll Associates.

"Paulette Pomerantz: Everything Became a Secret" from *Hiding to Survive: Stories of Jewish Children Rescued from the Holocaust.* © 1994 by Maxine B. Rosenberg. Reprinted by permission of Clarion Books/Houghton Mifflin Company. All rights reserved.

Text excerpt "Ordeal in the Owyhee Country" from *Women of Courage* by Margaret Truman, © 1976 by Margaret Truman Daniel. Reprinted by permission of William Morrow and Company, Inc.

"Middle Sister and the Tree" from *Ganekwane and the Green Dragon: Four Stories from Africa* by Corlia Fourie. Text © 1992 by Corlia Fourie. Used by permission of Albert Whitman & Company. All rights reserved. First published by Human & Rousseau (Pty) Ltd., Cape Town, South Africa.